Canada's Immigrants, Heroes and Countrymen

Robin Arthur
Sam Bayat

This book is dedicated to all those who stopped by at Canadian Legal Services in Dubai to make Canada their new home

Note to the Reader:

1. In order to provide a perspective of the political and economic paradigms that threatened the lives of peoples of the world and forced their flight out of their countries for refuge in Canada, the authors have submitted a historical commentary alongside the profiles of Canada's immigrants, heroes and countrymen. Those columns, with text italicized, must be read separately.
2. The reports on events or developments in recent years have not been specific to the year. For example, a reference to last year refers to 2000 or a reference to three years ago refers to 1998. This is based on the year of publication being 2001.

A publication of
Touch BASE
2099 Gottingen Street, Ste 201
Halifax, Nova Scotia,
B3K 3B2
Canada

ISBN : 0-9730000-0-7

Touch BASE gratefully acknowledges the copyright permission granted to Robin Arthur by Citizenship and Immigration Canada, for excerpts taken from its publication *Forging our Legacy: Canadian Citizenship and Immigration 1900-1977* and reproduced with the permission of the Minister of Public Works and Government Services Canada, 2001. These excerpts are reflected in the chapter: *Canada's First Immigrants*. It also gratefully acknowledges the copyright permission granted by Heirloom Publishing Inc, Ontario, for selected references made from their title "Canada at the Millennium - A Transcultural Society". These references are contained in the notes on the settlement of the Koreans and Indians in the big cities of Canada as well as the early immigration of East Europeans, namely, the Poles, Portuguese, Croatians and Hungarians.
Acknowledgement is also due to PIER 21 Society, the Sisters of Service, Kay Ruddick, a Red Cross escort after World War II, National Archives of Canada and Public Archives of Nova Scotia for permission to reproduce their photos.

References:

Voices in Exile Jurgen Hesse. Thinkware Publishers
Greeks: People of the Maritimes. Geraldine Thomas
Coming Canadians: Jean R. Burnet and Howard Palmer
The Book of Canadians. Carlotta Hacker. Hertig Publishers Ltd.
Under the Willow Tree: National Film Board of Canada

Foreword

The horrific terrorism unleashed on September 11 with attacks on the World Trade Centre's twin towers and the Pentagon in the United States brought into focus the need for greater vigilance at the borders as well as the introduction of legislation to pre-empt and deal with terrorism. Indeed, it is because Canada shares its borders with the United States, that it was deemed to be necessary for Canada, too, to review its immigration policy.

Be that as it may, Canada has reacted with some maturity and the crisis has not been blown out of proportion. It was being said then that this was not a good time to be a coloured person. The danger of painting all people of colour with the same brush was swiftly pre-empted by political leaders including Prime Minister Jean Chretien, who visited mosques and shared our belief that this is not a war on Islam or on Muslims but a war on terrorism.

But Canada has always been a country of immigrants and, historically, conflict in other parts of the world has sometimes tended to make Canadians somewhat wary about its citizens whose native origins have belonged in those countries. Besides slowing down the movement of newcomers to Canada, the First World War, for example, created difficulties for many foreign-born Canadians. Germans, who had previously ranked high on the list of desirable immigrants were not the only ones to suffer. Seen as enemy aliens because they had once been citizens of Germany or of the Austro-Hungarian Empire, Hungarians, Czechs, Romanians, Poles and Ukrainians also experienced hardship as a result of the war.

Later, when the Japanese bombed Pearl Harbour on December 7, 1941, Canada invoked the War Measures Act and stripped Japanese Canadians of their civil rights and ordered their removal from the West Coast. In the following year about 20,000 Japanese Canadians were dispatched to internment camps.

All that is now history. Despite the September 11 terror attacks, our government has reiterated the fact that Canada is and will continue to be a nation of immigrants. It recognizes the fact that Canadian identity will not be undermined by multiculturalism and that cultural pluralism is the very essence of Canadian identity.

It is, indeed, to that cause that this book is dedicated. *Canada's Immigrants, Heroes and Countrymen* tells the story of Canada's people since its early history. It pays tribute to Canadians who have done us proud in science and technology, in medicine, in discovery, adventure, sport, music and literature. It is an account of how our immigration policy has evolved over the last one hundred years.

In reviewing modern-day immigration to Canada, the book carries narratives on the political and economic conditions in Europe, South East Asia and Asia Pacific, Latin America, the Middle East and Africa, that drove people out of their countries to seek refuge in Canada and other parts of the world. The second World War, as everyone knows, was the primary cause of the current mass refugee phenomenon and now it's ethnic conflict that's blossoming on the stems of a new nationalism.

But the focus of this new title is people. It tells the stories of 65 new Canadians across Canada who have, as first generation immigrants, (the only exception to this being author Joy Kogawa and immigration lawyer Lee Cohen) achieved great success, demonstrated heroic courage in the transition process and who continue to give Canada their heart and soul. The people profiled include scientists, doctors and neurosurgeons, politicians, senators and even a former premier, sports heroes, authors, lawyers, journalists, businessmen, academics and so on.

It is, indeed, to them and to this nation of immigrants that this book pays tribute.

Robin Arthur
Sam Bayat

Canada's Immigrants, Heroes, Countrymen

Canada's early history is scarred by stories of land-grabbing, prejudiced treaties, the barbaric elimination of First Nation peoples, ugly Anglo-French battles and, up until the middle of the twentieth century, the perpetuation of race-driven legislation. The segregation of Chinese schools, the isolation of its citizens of Japanese descent after the bombing of Pearl Harbour during World War II or the infamous "continuous journey" regulation to bar East Indian emigration to Canada are some of those many scars. But Canadians cannot be nailed to a guilt cross forever. Canada is making amends.

Canada, with a Charter that guarantees rights and freedoms to all Canadians today, regardless of race or faith, is truly becoming a template for the model state. It's political role on the world stage and its commitment to be a peacekeeper, rather than an aggressor, make it stand out from the comity of nations. It has thrown its weight behind UN conventions that have addressed the problems of war-displaced refugees and is a champion of human rights.

War and conflict in the last couple of decades have challenged host countries like Canada to accept more refugees per year now than ever before. At the beginning of the new millennium, the worldwide refugee count was at about 22.3 million, up by about a million from January 1 of 1999. As anyone would know, the conflicts in Kosovo and the Balkan region triggered the whopping increase. Looking back over the preceding decade, in 1990 the UNHCR (United Nations High Commission on Refugees) was helping an estimated 15 million people – that was before hostilities in northern Iraq, the former Yugoslavia, Rwanda and Africa's Great Lakes region had broken out. The series of major crises took the refugee count to an all-time high of 27 million in 1995 before gradually tapering off at the end of the century. Canada has stood shoulder to shoulder with the UN agency to absorb its share of the refugee population committed under its obligation to the 1951 Geneva Convention on the status of refugees and its 1967 Protocol to which it is a signatory.

The UNHCR considers Canada's independent, quasi-judicial Immigration and Refugee Board (IRB) to be an exemplary national status determination mechanism. In 1998, at least 24,000 people requested refugee status in Canada. The IRB granted it, in 12,880 of the 23,200 cases decided, achieving an approval rate of 55.5 per cent. The Government's target for resettlement this year is close to about 11,000. Canada is also a forerunner in several recent diplomatic initiatives including the Convention banning anti-personnel landmines, the International Criminal Court and the entire human security agenda.

This new face of Canada contrasts sharply with the face it wanted to sport a hundred years ago. So in a sense, this national evolution has not been without its share of problems. Throughout these one hundred years, Canada's immigration laws have tended to reflect strong public opinion. When Clifford Sifton, the Minister of the Interior in Wilfred Laurel's government in 1896 turned to the United States for recruiting farmers, the legislation kept out blacks for they were widely regarded as being cursed with the burden of their African ancestry. When unsubstantiated rumours broke out of the imminent invasion of Canada by forces of German-Americans during the Austro-Hungarian war, the doors were closed to immigration for the Magyars. The Vancouver Riots in 1907 were also stirred by opposition from Canadians to Asian immigration.

But there comes a time in a nation's history when one man or woman is thrust upon it to change its course. It was just as well that reform by Ellen Fairclough, the minister of immigration in John Diefenbaker's government in the 1960s brought that wind of change. On January 19, 1962 Fairclough tabled new regulations in the House that virtually eliminated racial discrimination as a major feature of Canada's immigration policy. When the new regulations were implemented on February 1, 1962, Canada became the first of the three large receiving countries in international migration - the other two being the United States and Australia - to dismantle its discriminatory immigration policy. In tandem, Prime Minister, John Diefenbaker's cherished Canadian Bill of Rights (1960) had rejected discrimination by reason of race, colour, national origin, religion, or sex.

In the later part of the sixties, Robert Andras, the Minister of Manpower and Immigration in Prime Minister Pierre Trudeau's administration (1968-1972) called a referendum to find an answer to the basic question: "Why do we have immigration to this country?" That referendum finally broke new ground resulting in the Immigration Act of 1976 – the cornerstone of present day immigration policy which sought to be race-free, skills-driven, pragmatic yet sympathetic and humanitarian. Andras' referendum underpinned immigration as an economic reality that injects skills into the workforce and spurs consumption into the markets to grow the economy.

Canada's leadership in the later half of the twentieth century, indeed, changed the narrow thinking that marked Canadian life in the preceding decades. In the evolutionary process, Canada opened its windows to the world. Since the post-war rise in immigration and the opening of its gates to the world's displaced people, it welcomed refugees from Hungary, Palestine, Uganda, Vietnam. The removal of factors of race in the immigration policy through the introduction of the Points System opened the floodgates to emigration out of Asia.

About a million immigrants came to Canada in the first half of the nineties according to the 1996 census. The immigrant tide has forced a sea-change in the demographics. Today's new immigrants come from Hong Kong, India, China, Taiwan. Pakistan, Philippines, Iran, Sri Lanka and of course, from the United States and the UK. They account for half the total that immigrates to Canada every year. At the same time traditional sources of immigrants, notably Europe and more recently South Asia, are giving way to Latin America, China, West Asia and Africa. By the end of the current decade, stats say 80 per cent of all immigrants could be visible minorities.

In this process of change, Canada is coming to grips with its identity crisis. Although a *Multiculturalism Act* is in place, Canadians are divided over whether or not a nation can project a league of many cultures within one framework. Douglas Fischer writing in the *Toronto Sun* observes: "How can we sustain some unity of purpose and a sense of a whole community if we project a league of national cultures within one framework. You and me and our children have enough to do with the basic problem of the French and English duality, without enshrining the whole world's diversity within our history and borders." His observation contrasts significantly with a federal government statement which notes: "Canadian identity will not be undermined by multiculturalism. Indeed, we believe that cultural pluralism is the very essence of Canadian identity." Kirk Watson writing in *Canadian Overtones* has also made a worthy observation: "Our national attitude towards immigrants of non-British origin has already passed through two ignorant and discreditable phases," he says. "I foresee a future Canada in which every individual would be inspired to fuller citizenship by the realization of his origin."

Canadians who do us proud

Canada is justifiably proud of the many great people it has given the world – the world's greatest brain surgeons, the inventor of insulin, the fog horn and the telephone, the great master of jazz, the world's most respected economist, sports heroes that have made hockey history and men of great courage. Canada's 20th century scientific community, for example, owes much to the foundation created by John William Dawson (1820-1899), the first Canadian-born scientist of worldwide reputation. Canada is proud of Hungarian-born John Korda (1929), a satellite researcher who was a key player in the development of Canada's long-term space plans. The world also owes much to Dr. John Fitz Gerald who set up the laboratory that for the first time mass-produced insulin during the 1920s. German-born Gerhard Herzberg (1904) did Canada proud when he won the Nobel Prize in Chemistry, for his pioneering work on molecular spectroscopy – which studies light emitted or absorbed by molecules.

Canada has given the world a string of medical geniuses too. Wilder Penfield (1891-1976) was one of the world's greatest brain surgeons, whose research led to the finding that epilepsy could be controlled if damaged brain tissue is removed after an attack. Wilfred Bigelow (1913) is recognized as one of the world's leading heart surgeons and the inventor of the pacemaker - a device that jumpstarts a stopped heart. C. Miller Fisher, a prisoner of war in Germany after the ship on which he was medical officer was sunk in the south Atlantic, told the world that the carotid artery was the cause of strokes. Daniel David Palmer, a 50-year old immigrant began the practice of chiropractic - the healing art - in 1895 and devoted his entire life to establishing it as a rational science and philosophy.

Canada's heroes are inventors too. It gave the world Alexander Graham Bell (1847-1922), the inventor of the telephone. It's proud of Armand Bombardier (1907-1964) the inventor of the snowmobile as well as of Reginald Fessenden (1866-1932) the man who invented the radio - transmitting actual sounds and not wireless messages through the Morse code. It was home to Sanford Fleming, (1827-1915) the inventor of Standard Time (which divides the world into 24 time zones); Robert Foulis (1796-1866) the inventor of the steam fog-horn, Abraham Gesner, the inventor of kerosene, a light oil used as fuel for lamps. Canadians credited with discoveries include, among others, John Williamson (1907-1958) who discovered one of the world's richest diamond deposits in Tanganyika (Tanzania) in Africa; Thomas Wilson (1860-1915) who discovered how carbide and acetylene are made combining lime and coal tar and Master mariner Joseph Elzier Bernier who explored and mapped the

Arctic and in 1909 proclaimed the Arctic Islands of Canada to the world.

Canadians have demonstrated outstanding bravery whether in adventure or in war. Casey Baldwin *(1882-1948*) was the first Canadian and the seventh person in the world to fly an airplane. Crowfoot (1830-1890) was the celebrated Blackfoot chief who became famous for his outstanding bravery during the guerrilla warfare on the prairies. Jacques Dextraze (1919) gained fame for his 1944 assault on a contingent of Germans in Normandy. He later served in the Korean War and in the sixties commanded the United Nations forces in the Congo. William Hall (1827-1904) the son of a slave brought to Halifax during the war of 1812 was one of the very earliest Canadians to win the Victoria Cross. Hall became a hero in 1857 when he rescued the beleaguered British garrison besieged at Lucknow in India. Charles de Salaberry (1778-1829) became the hero of the war of 1812, when he routed the American forces which invaded Lower Canada.

In sport, Canada is on the fast track. Wayne Gretzky (1961) who made hockey history, has been acclaimed as the greatest, the youngest, the best. Rocket Richard (1921) played in more than a thousand games for the Montreal Canadiens, winning eight Stanley Cups. Sharif Khan (1945) born in Pakistan, is regarded as the king of squash. Angela Taylor (1958) born in Jamaica, Canada's fastest woman sprinter at the time, ran to victory in the 1982 Commonwealth Games. Steve Podborski (1957) was proclaimed king of the mountains after winning the men's World Cup downhill skiing championship in 1982. James Naismith (1861-1939) invented the game of basketball. Tommy Burns, of German descent (born Noah Brusso), was the first and only Canadian to hold the world heavy weight boxing title in 1906

Other Canadian heroes are like music to the ears : Andre Gagnon (1942) the concert pianist and composer. Oscar Peterson (1925) one of the great masters of jazz. Paul Anka, of Diana fame, which sold five million copies. Tom Connors (1936), who wrote his first song at 11 and since has written more than 500 songs and cut over 30 LPs. Ann Murray (1945) of "Snowbird" fame and who has charmed fans across the world; Emma Albani and so many others.

On the political stage, a fine crop of Canadians have steered Canada's progress at home as well as in the comity of nations. John A. Macdonald (1815-1891) Canada's first prime minister was the man who brought about confederation and made it a functioning country by building the Canadian Pacific Railway across it. He was brought to Canada as a child and raised in Kingston. Lester B. Pearson (1897-1972) negotiated Canada's entry into NATO, served as president of the UN General Assembly and proposed a peacekeeping force in the Middle East thus pre-empting the Suez crisis. Joey Smallwood (1900) brought Newfoundland into Confederation in 1949. Pierre Elliot Trudeau (1919-2000) who was swept into office of the Prime Minister in the sixties for a term that lasted 15 years takes credit for the patriation of Canada's constitution as well as for the other pieces of legislation on Biculturalism and Bilingualism.

Canada's literary fame has been steered by people like L.M. Montgomery (1874-1942) the author of Anne of Green Gables; Sri-Lanka born Michael Ondaatje (1943) who gained fame for his volumes of verse, and his novel *The English Patient*; Margaret Atwood - winner of the Booker Prize - who first gained fame with her poetry collection *The Circle Game* and later with *The Edible Woman* and *Survival;* Czechoslovakia-born Josef Skvorecky (1924) who was nominated for the Nobel Prize in Literature, although all his best known books, *The Cowards* and *The Bass Saxophone,* were banned in his native country; and John Kenneth Galbraith (1908) one of the world's leading economists and author of the international bestseller *The Affluent Society*.

Canada is proud too of people such as David Suzuki (1936) a geneticist and scientist who through his radio and TV programs introduced scientific concepts to the people of Canada as well as of Shizuye Takashima (1928) who like Suzuki, although born of Canadian-born parents, was interned in camps during World War II when Canada was at war with Japan. Takashima is author of the book *A Child in Prison Camp* which describes her experiences during World War II. Finally, Canada is proud too of Russian-born Jan Zurakowski (1914) who became Canada's famous test pilot who first piloted a plane at the age of 15. He was raised in Poland but escaped to Britain when Germany invaded it and joined the Royal Air Force. He immigrated to Canada in 1952.

Canada's first immigrants

The reports of Viking voyages around AD 1000 are a divergence from the emphasis on French and British explorers in Canadian history. The Germans, Italians, Portuguese, the Slavs and Greeks and even the Chinese figure in exploration reports. A German named Tyrkier, was reportedly part of the Viking expedition of AD 1001 and archaeological finds at L'Anse aux Meadows in Newfoundland appear to confirm that fact. Furthermore two German skippers, Diedrich Pining and Hans Pothorst – in the Danish service, may have rediscovered Newfoundland and Labrador between 1471 and 1480 and a German who was on Sir Humphrey Gilbert's expedition is reported to have set foot in Newfoundland in 1583.

The Italians also claim that Verazzano originally of Florence, explored the coast of Nova Scotia in 1524 and provided some new insights. The Portuguese point to considerable activity in the North Atlantic in the Fifteenth century, when Diogo de Tervi's expedition in 1452 is said to have provided information for Christopher Columbus. Poles and Croats claim to have participated in early explorations. A Pole is said to have discovered Labrador in 1476.

The Chinese tell tales of Buddhist monks who sailed from China on rafts and went ashore in AD 458 establishing settlements in Vancouver in 499. The Greeks and the Spanish tell of a visit to the West Coast by Juan de Fuca, who was Greek by birth but was navigating for the Spanish navy in 1592.

Although the French and the British took possession of the northern parts of Canada, establishing the first settlements in 1605, many countries nonetheless were represented in the colony, including those in Europe, China and Africa. The English (especially prisoners and refugees from New England), Irish and Scots were the most numerous.

Africans had settled from the early seventeenth century. The first African to have been brought to New France directly from Madagascar in

Africa was Olivier le Jeune. He is reported to have died a free man in 1654. Blacks came with early settlers and later in groups either as fugitives or as free men. In 1793 Lieutenant Governor John Graves Simcoe, who opposed slavery introduced a bill in the assembly for its gradual abolition and by 1860 there may have been as many as 40,000 blacks in Canada.

The earliest evidence of European exploration can be seen from Norse runes - the stone carvings - found in the south east corner of Nova Scotia. This settlement is thought to have occurred about 950 A.D when the Viking voyages brought Norsemen to the region. The settlement of Leif Ericsson at Vinland in 1001 is evidenced at L'Anse aux Meadows, north of Newfoundland.

Almost five hundred years later, John Cabot became the first European to discover North America. He made two voyages between 1497 and 1498 and his landfall was reported to be a stone's throw away from Leif Ericsson's settlement. Cabot will be remembered because he was the first man to discover and tell about the mainland of North America. England claimed all of North America because Cabot had discovered it for her before the French and Spanish. But nobody knows where exactly Cabot landed. It could have been Newfoundland or Cape Breton.

The Italians and Portuguese were among the other European settlers that travelled to the continent before the British and French laid claim to North America. In 1524, Giovanni da Verrazzano, an Italian mariner is reported to have come to Newfoundland and applied the name Arcadia to the site of Kitty Hawk, North Carolina. In 1520 Joao Alvarez Fagundes, a Portuguese navigator, sailed along the south coast of Newfoundland and into the Gulf of Saint Lawrence and began a settlement at Ingonish in Cape Breton.

Nova Scotia reports the second oldest permanent settlement in North America at Annapolis Royal. The fur traders in France had to be persuaded to settle in the strange wilderness that North America was at the beginning of Sixteenth century. The King of France believed that if French settlements were made, he would have a stronger claim to the country and so in 1600 he promised trading rights to a group if they would take settlers to live in America. Consequently, the sole right to trade in Acadia was given to a French nobleman named Sieur de Monts. In exchange for this right, De Monts and his company were to bring out settlers to live on his lands and priests to convert Indians to Christianity. In 1604 De Monts, Champlain, Poutrincourt and some others crossed the Atlantic into Acadia - the name given to the Maritimes.

The first one hundred years of the Irish presence in Nova Scotia are reported to have been ones of great courage and achievement for a "warm-hearted people who came in poverty" The arrival of the ship *Hector* at Pictou in 1773 marked the beginning of a fairly sustained period of Scottish immigration, which lasted - at least in Cape Breton - until the mid-nineteenth century. The Scottish presence in Nova Scotia eventually meant a challenge to the English-Anglican hierarchy. Those who came during the eighteenth century were mainly voluntary immigrants seeking to improve upon the economic conditions they knew in Scotland.

Canada's first great wave of immigration

Canada's first great wave of European immigration followed a lacklustre period in its immigration history. Despite the best efforts of Sir John A. Macdonald's Conservative government to attract newcomers, large-scale immigration failed to become a reality in the first three decades after Confederation in 1867. Canada's immigration prospects only started to look up in the 1890s. Fortunately for Canada, the reinvigorated economy coincided with a population explosion in Europe and a rapidly dwindling supply of good free land in the United States. Then, too, there was the election of Sir Wilfrid Laurier's Liberal government in 1896, which immediately launched an aggressive campaign to encourage settlement of the West.

Clifford Sifton and his policies

The principal planner and promoter of the campaign for western settlement was Clifford Sifton, who was determined to fill the empty Prairies with suitable farmers as rapidly as possible. Having always been a provincial booster, the new Minister had unbounded confidence in the West.

Furthermore, he was firmly convinced that massive agricultural immigration was the key to Canadian prosperity. He then simplified the regulations of the *Dominion Lands Act,* the 1872 piece of legislation that granted a quarter section of free land (160 acres or 64.7 hectares) to any settler 21 years of age or older who paid a ten-dollar registration fee, lived on his quarter section for three years, cultivated 30 acres (12.1 hectares), and built a permanent dwelling.

In his quest for suitable agriculturalists to farm the West, however, Clifford Sifton stressed new fields for recruiting immigrants. One of these was the United States.

Estimates indicate that between 1901 and 1914, over 750,000 immigrants entered Canada from the United States.

No welcome mat for Black Africans

When it came to prospective American settlers, the Immigration Branch solicited only white farmers. No attempt was made to recruit black agriculturalists, for they were widely regarded as being cursed with the burden of their African ancestry. In its attempts to exclude black settlers, the Immigration Branch undoubtedly reflected public opinion in the West and elsewhere in Canada. Thousands of free black people had been among the Loyalists who had settled in Nova Scotia in 1783. Later, runaway slaves from the United States had obtained refuge in Canada. On learning that anti-black sentiment in the newly created state of Oklahoma threatened to drive a large migration of black Americans north to the Edmonton area, the citizens of Alberta's capital mounted a strong protest against the immigration of blacks. The anti-black backlash in Western Canada played directly into the hands of Immigration Branch officials who wanted to see the Canadian border closed to black immigration. Accordingly, in 1911 these officials took unprecedented steps to have Canada acquire an exclusion ordinance against black settlers.

The Ukrainians

In his urgent search for farm labourers, the new Minister was prepared to admit agriculturalists from places other than Great Britain, the United States, and northern Europe, long the preferred suppliers of immigrants for Canada. The vast majority of English-speaking Canadians deplored the idea of Canada's admitting "illiterate Slavs in overwhelming numbers."

Nevertheless, by dint of his forceful personality, status, and determination, Sifton managed to proceed with his controversial plan. The Ukrainians were by far the largest group to immigrate to Canada from eastern and central Europe in these years. Between 1891, when the first wave of Ukrainian immigrants came to Canada and the outbreak of the First World War, approximately 170,000 Ukrainians settled in this country, attracted by the offer of free land, a sense of space, and an opportunity to make a living in a free and open society.

For the most part, these Ukrainian newcomers were small farmers and labourers from Galicia and Bukovina who were fleeing oppressive social and economic conditions in their homeland. Commonly called Galicians, they headed for those parts of the West that provided meadow, water, wood, and, if possible, contact with pioneers who spoke their language. As a result, large numbers of Ukrainians settled in the Prairie provinces, from southeastern Manitoba through central Saskatchewan to the Rocky Mountain foothills west of Edmonton.

The Germans

Among the thousands of immigrants who homesteaded on the Prairies in these years were settlers of German origin. Most came not from the German Empire, but from the Russian and the Austro-Hungarian empires and the Balkan countries, where German colonies had been established in the eighteenth century. The growing class of landless workers and a dearth of factory jobs also spurred the exodus. From the 1890s until the outbreak of the First World War, approximately 35,000 Germans settled in Manitoba, representing 7.5 percent of that province's total population. Most settlements in Saskatchewan broke down along denominational lines.

At the base of German immigration to Canada were those brave men and women who travelled across the Atlantic from Europe to colonial Halifax in September 1750 on the ship *Anne*. The authorities housed and employed the new settlers for three years in Halifax and Dartmouth until the majority were removed to found Lunenburg town in 1753. There, in Lunenburg, they took to boat building and fishing. In 1995 their legacy was honoured when UNESCO declared Lunenburg a World Heritage Site.

The German settlers, many of them Mennonites, that came between 1792 and 1837 sought not only free land but also religious freedom and exemption from military service. They founded communities in the Niagara district and also contributed to the growth and industrial development of the Grand River settlement.

The Italians

Canada did not actively seek Italian immigrants in this period because Clifford Sifton considered Italians ill-fitted for pioneering. Most were peasants or sharecroppers, small landowners, and rural day labourers from the impoverished southern regions of Italy, where they had wrested a living from a harsh environment and struggled against an exploitative socio-economic order.

From among those who arrived in Canada, thousands went to work for this country's railways. Others found employment in the mining industry, where there was a demand for intensive labour. Some 3,000 Italians arrived in Montréal in 1904, and two years later, when construction of the trunk lines of the Grand Trunk Pacific, the Canadian Northern, and the National Transcontinental railways began in earnest, there was a further dramatic increase in the numbers of Italians coming to Canada.

The Russians

The first great wave of European immigration to Canada included the first Russians to settle in the country. They were Doukhobors, members of a peasant sect whose pacifism and communal lifestyle had invited czarist authorities to mount a campaign of brutal persecution and harassment against them. Fortunately for the Doukhobors, their plight aroused the sympathy of Leo Tolstoy, the great Russian novelist, who used his fame to help them to emigrate. In late January 1899, the first of five parties of Doukhobors, numbering over 7,500 people, settled in the Prince Albert and Yorkton areas in what is now the province of Saskatchewan.

The Doukhobors, however, refused to have any dealings with the state. They refused to take the oath of allegiance, and they would not register births, marriages, and deaths; neither would they allow their children to be educated in the public system. These were widened by the actions of an extremist group, the Sons of Freedom, who liberated cattle, burnt property, and refused to till the land. Order was finally restored by the Doukhobors' spiritual leader Peter Veregin.

After arriving in the Northwest Territories in 1903, he quickly set about reorganizing the sect members into a prosperous farming community and keeping the Sons of Freedom under control. In 1908, Veregin purchased a large tract of land in British Columbia (the oath of allegiance was not a requirement in that province), organized the Doukhobors as the Christian Community of Universal Brotherhood, and established community villages in the province.

The British

Although there were relatively few good agriculturalists left to court in the "mother country," the Canadian government continued to promote immigration from the United Kingdom, principally because English Canadians took it for granted that their federal government would do everything possible to retain the British character of the country. Most British newcomers in this pre-war period emigrated to Canada in hopes of finding a higher standard of living and freedom from the rigidities of the hallowed British class system.

Included in the ranks of these non-sponsored immigrants were not only people of modest means but also individuals with substantial funds who would often invest in large-scale ranching or farming ventures in Western Canada. The great influx from Britain in these years also included poor immigrants who had been assisted by charitable organizations wanting to rid the United Kingdom of paupers and help them make a fresh start in the colonies. One of the many philanthropic agencies involved in this endeavour was the Salvation Army, which was established in Canada in 1882.

The Japanese

As British Columbia faced the Pacific Ocean, it drew many of its non-British newcomers from Asia, including Japan. Japanese immigrants did not begin arriving in appreciable numbers until 1900. By 1914, however, only 10,000 Japanese had settled in the whole of Canada, by far the largest number in British Columbia.

The first wave of Japanese immigrants, called Issei, arrived between 1877 and 1928. Prior to 1907, most Japanese settlers were young men. In that year, at Canada's insistence, Japan limited the number of males who could emigrate to this country to 400 a year, thereby becoming the only nation to specifically control the movement of its people to Canada.

The Issei were invariably young and came from poor and overcrowded fishing and farming villages on the islands of Honshu and Kyushu. Most settled in or near Vancouver and Victoria, in fishing villages and pulp towns along the Pacific coast, and on farms in the Fraser Valley.

The Sikhs

The first immigrants from India came to Vancouver and Victoria in 1904. Although British Columbia did its best to discourage non-white immigrants from Asia, barring them from the professions and denying them the right to vote, among other measures, some 5,000 immigrants from India had journeyed to the province by the end of 1907. Of these, the overwhelming majority were Sikhs.

The first Sikhs arrived in the province in 1904, having learned about its beauties and advantages from a detachment of Sikh soldiers who had returned home from London by way of Canada after attending Queen Victoria's Diamond Jubilee in 1897. Most of these early Sikh immigrants found work in the province's lumber mills and logging camps.

In 1999, a postage stamp was issued to commemorate the contributions that Sikh Canadians had made in the building of Canada. Among those present at the unveiling ceremony was Herb Dhaliwal, then the Minister of National Revenue, whose Sikh grandfather had come to Canada in 1906.

Changing direction

No sooner had Frank Oliver become Minister of the Interior than he set about making immigration policy more restrictive. Two Acts capped his legislative program, the first being the *Immigration Act* of 1906 and the second being the *Immigration Act* of 1910.

The Immigration Act of 1906

Besides defining "an immigrant," this Act barred a broad spectrum of individuals and increased the government's power to deport certain classes of immigrants. It also decreed the amount of "landing money" immigrants needed to have in their possession on arrival and provided for the establishment of controls along the Canada-United States border. There had been laws since 1869 prohibiting certain kinds of immigration and since 1889 allowing designated classes of immigrants to be returned whence they came. The 1906 Act differed in degree, significantly increasing the number of categories of prohibited immigrants and officially sanctioning the deportation of undesirable newcomers.

The proposed Act inspired considerable debate in the House of Commons, much of it concerning the definition of an immigrant and the provision for a head tax on immigrants: a tax to be paid by each immigrant on being admitted to Canada. Sweeping aside all the technicalities, though, this parliamentary discussion revealed two basic views about the general direction that immigration should take.

Among those who felt that immigration barriers should be raised was the provincial chief of the Conservatives, Frederick Monk, who thought that Canada should emulate the example of the United States and impose a head tax on immigrants. By contrast, W.M. German, the Liberal member from Welland, lobbied for an open-door policy. Not surprisingly, German's stance on immigration found favour with Canadian industrialists, who lobbied for a continuous stream of immigrants willing to work long hours for low pay.

The Immigration Act of 1910

The second milestone in restrictive immigration legislation was reached in 1910. The *Immigration Act* of 1910, unlike the 1906 Act, conferred on the Cabinet the authority to exclude "immigrants belonging to any race deemed unsuited to the climate or requirements of Canada." The Act also strengthened the government's power to deport individuals, such as anarchists, on the grounds of political and moral instability.

In its determination to discourage the entry of certain categories of people, the government introduced still other measures. It passed an order-in council, for example, requiring immigrants of Asian origin to have $200 in cash at the time of landing, a formidable sum in those days when it is realized that in 1910, the average production worker in Canada took home only $417 in annual wages.

The Vancouver Riot of 1907

In the course of promoting British and American immigration, Frank Oliver moved further along the path of selective immigration. Several developments conspired to push him in this direction, one being the Vancouver Riot of September 1907. The riot, which resulted in extensive damage to buildings occupied by Orientals, was precipitated by a rock hurled by a youngster through the window of a Chinese store following a giant anti-Asian parade.

Although the rampage ignited spontaneously, it had complex origins. The riot's principal roots lay deep in an anti-Asian sentiment that had been smouldering for years in British Columbia. This racial antipathy reached new heights in 1907 when it was reported that the Grand Trunk Pacific Railway was planning to import thousands of Japanese labourers to work on the completion of the railway's western leg. To add to the tension, over 2,300 Japanese arrived in the province in July alone, far more than had been anticipated.

With Japanese immigration soaring to unprecedented levels, the perception grew among West Coast whites that the Japanese had become the leading Oriental threat to their province's cultural integrity. The Japanese, like the Chinese, had always been regarded as inassimilable, but after Japan's victory over Russia in the Russo-Japanese War (1905) the Japanese image took on an even more frightening dimension.

As alarm mounted over the Japanese influx, hysterical comment about the Japanese "invasion" appeared in the daily press. Accompanying these expressed fears were demands by the Vancouver Trades and Labour Council for measures to stem the rising immigrant tide. Not content to work within the political process alone, the council formed the Asiatic Exclusion League. The league subsequently broke all ties with the Trades and Labour Council and staged the anti-Asian parade that preceded the Vancouver Riot of 1907.

Following the riot, the Laurier government found itself in the seemingly untenable position of having to placate British Columbia and Japan simultaneously. The solution lay in compromise. In response to British Columbia's insistent demands that Asian immigration be halted,

Ottawa negotiated an agreement with Japan whereby Japan would voluntarily limit the emigration of Japanese to Canada to 400 a year.

Once the Japanese claims were settled, Mackenzie King, the Deputy Minister of Labour and a future Prime Minister, sought to determine the origins of the recent Oriental influx. In his report, he attributed the abnormally large numbers to high immigration from Hawaii and to the activities of immigration companies based in Canada. King concluded that immigration by way of Hawaii should be banned, that companies should be prohibited from importing contract labour, and that Ottawa should severely limit the admission of Japanese newcomers. He also implied that immigration from India should be discouraged.

In response to King's findings, the Laurier government made an important amendment to the *Immigration Act.* This amendment, which came into effect in 1908, was known as the "continuous-journey regulation." Under this regulation, all would-be immigrants were required to travel to Canada by continuous passage from their country of origin or citizenship on a through-ticket purchased in that country. Since no shipping company provided direct service from India to Canada, this ingenious device served to ban all Indian immigration. It also closed the door on the Hawaii route for Japanese immigration.

The Komagata Maru incident

The continuous-journey regulation and subsequent barriers to East Indian immigration did not go unchallenged. The most dramatic challenge occurred on 23 May 1914, when 376 East Indians (22 were returning Canadian residents) arrived in Vancouver harbour on board the *Komagata Maru,* a Japanese tramp steamer hired by a wealthy Sikh merchant and former labour contractor from Hong Kong, Gurdit Singh Sarhali. The steamer met with an unmitigatedly hostile reception. A week later the case of Munshi Singh, a young Sikh farmer, was heard and he was ruled inadmissible on the grounds that he had violated three Orders in Council, in particular the continuous-journey regulation.

When the B.C. Court of Appeal upheld the refusal of a lower court to order his release, the way was paved for Munshi Singh and all the remaining passengers to be deported. The steamer then sailed to India, having left behind just a handful of passengers, previous residents of British Columbia who had been allowed to land by the federal government. Sikh political pressure finally persuaded the federal government to pass an Order in Council in 1919 allowing "British Hindus residing in Canada" to bring their wives and children to this country. The detested continuous-journey regulation remained in effect, however, until 1947.

The First World War and foreign-born Canadians

Besides slowing down the movement of newcomers to Canada, the First World War created difficulties for many foreign-born Canadians. Germans, who had previously ranked high on the list of desirable immigrants, were not the only ones to suffer. Deemed enemy aliens because they had once been citizens of Germany or of the Austro-Hungarian Empire, Hungarians, Czechs, Romanians, Poles, and Ukrainians also experienced hardship as a result of the war. Unsubstantiated rumours of imminent invasions of Canada by large forces of German-Americans increased Canadian anxiety about foreigners in their midst. This uneasiness was further heightened by an incautious statement made by a Winnipeg prelate, Bishop Nykyta Budka. On 27 July 1914, while the world anxiously awaited Austria's response to the assassination of the Archduke Francis Ferdinand, the bishop urged his Ukrainian parishioners to remember their duty to the Austro-Hungarian Empire if war should occur and to hasten to the defence of the threatened fatherland.

Jewish immigration

Although immigration to Canada between 1919 and 1925 was largely restricted to newcomers from Canada’s traditional source countries, there were two notable exceptions. One involved the Russian Mennonites, the other, Jews. Even though the Department of Immigration and Colonization was generally hostile to the idea of admitting Jews, placing various impediments in their way, approximately 40,000 Jews did succeed in entering this country during the interwar period, most being admitted by special permit. Among these Jews were 200 war orphans. In 1923, the Canadian government agreed to admit 5,000 Jewish refugees who had fled from Russia to Romania between 1918 and 1920 and had subsequently been ordered to leave their adopted country.

If the Railway Agreement of 1925 led to a surge in the influx of newcomers from continental Europe, the Great Depression of the 1930s succeeded in choking off almost all immigration to Canada. During these years of economic devastation and widespread unemployment, the federal government strove hard to seal off Canada not only to prospective immigrants but also to refugees fleeing Nazi Germany, particularly Jewish refugees. There can be no doubt that Ottawa's restrictive legislation reflected the general Canadian attitude towards immigration, for Canadians across the country took the view that immigrants threatened scarce jobs in an economy that in 1933 saw almost one-quarter of the labour force unemployed.

Among those barred from entering Canada during the 1930s were thousands of desperate refugees, many of them Jews fleeing persecution at the hands of the Nazis. The persecution of the Jews was particularly savage, especially after the German invasion of Austria in March 1938. Thousands of the Jews who managed to escape the Nazi tide sought refuge in Canada, but by and large their appeals were ignored. Anti-Semitism was rife throughout Canada, where, in some places, Jews could not hold particular jobs, own property, or stay in certain hotels. It was most strident in Quebec.

Champions of the oppressed

As dismal as this picture appears, there were in fact many Canadians who opposed the government's policy and wanted to see immigration barriers lowered. In addition to members of pro-refugee organizations and leading spokespeople for the Jewish community, they included prominent members of the Protestant churches, newspaper editors and commentators in English-speaking Canada, and members of the Co-operative Commonwealth Federation, particularly its leader, M.J. Coldwell. Foremost among the non-sectarian refugee lobbies was the Canadian National Committee on Refugees.

Post-war rise in immigration

The *Canadian Citizenship Act* of 1947 coincided with a post-war rise in immigration. Notable among the new arrivals to Canadian shores in the early post-war period were British war brides who had married members of Canada's fighting forces. During and after the war, some 48,000 of them arrived in this country.

To its credit, Canada decided to admit displaced persons even before the international community had reached an agreement on the permanent resettlement of hundreds of thousands of Europe's homeless. Nearly 250,000 displaced persons and other refugees were admitted to Canada between 1947 and 1962.

Of the 165,000 refugees who entered this country between 1947 and 1953, Poles comprised the largest group. In descending order of numerical strength were Ukrainians, Germans and Austrians, Jews, Latvians Lithuanians, Hungarians, Czechs, Dutch, and Russians.

All told, these groups comprised 86 percent of the Europeans allowed to enter Canada in this period.

A further liberalization of immigration policy

The government, in June 1950, issued an Order in Council that replaced all former Orders in Council and amendments with respect to immigration; retained the preference for British, Irish, French, and American immigrants and widened the admissible classes of European immigrants to include any healthy applicant of good character who had skills needed in Canada and who could easily integrate into Canadian society. Later in the year regulations were changed to allow the entry of additional categories of Asians. In a further move, the government took German immigrants off the enemy-alien list - Italian immigrants had been removed from the list in 1947- as a result, Germans joined swelling numbers of Italians in applying for admission to Canada.

The 1952 Immigration Act

A long-awaited new *Immigration Act,* the first since 1910 was finally enacted by Parliament in 1952. One of the Act's most significant provisions vested a large degree of uncontrolled discretionary power in the Minister and his or her officials. Jack Pickersgill was one Minister who employed the Act compassionately and to good purpose. On different occasions he waived immigration regulations and approved the admission, under minister's permit, of epileptics whose condition could be controlled by drugs, tubercular cases, and people who had a previous history of mental illness, provided these cases posed no danger to the community and were adequately sponsored.

Refugees from Palestine

When Pickersgill was at the helm of Citizenship and Immigration, Canada took the bold step of admitting some Palestinian Arabs, driven from their homeland by the Israeli-Arab war of 1948. In 1955, when the idea for the scheme was conceived, over 900,000 Palestinian refugees were living in Syria, Lebanon, Jordan, and Gaza. The resettlement of these refugees abroad was nothing if not a politically explosive issue in the Middle East.

By participating in the operation Canada risked incurring the wrath of Arabs, who might charge that it was part of a Zionist plot to remove Palestinian refugees from the care they received from the United Nations Relief and Rehabilitation Administration (UNRRA) and deprive them of their right to return to Palestine.

Nevertheless, in 1955, a young official at the Canadian legation in Beirut, Lebanon, where UNRRA had its headquarters, approached the agency and obtained its co-operation in arranging for a selection of Palestinian refugees to be interviewed by a Canadian immigration team.

In sharp contrast to the attention given its admission of the Palestinian refugees, Canada's admission of close to 38,000 Hungarian refugees in 1956 attracted a great deal of coverage over the years. This country's response to the desperate situation of the Hungarian refugees represents one of the few times in Canadian history when Canadians have whole-heartedly welcomed immigrants. In fact, of all the states that accepted Hungarian refugees for permanent resettlement, none surpassed Canada in its generosity. They can be attributed directly to the pressure created by the Canadian public, whose sympathies were aroused by the plight of over 200,000 Hungarians fleeing their homeland after Russian tanks brutally crushed the Hungarian uprising in 1956.

The new wave of immigrants

Unlike the newcomers in the earlier boom period of Canadian immigration (1900-1914), those who arrived in the late 1940s and 1950s were a more heterogeneous body, with a greater diversity of skills, training, and occupations. By 1957, the year that marked the end of the post-war boom period in Canadian immigration, Canada, which now included Newfoundland, boasted a population of 16.6 million and ranked as a major industrial nation, with manufacturing providing its major source of income and employment. It was therefore the urbanized and industrialized provinces - Ontario, Quebec, Alberta, and British Columbia - that benefited most from immigration. Now the majority of new arrivals came from continental Europe, especially Germany, Italy, and the Netherlands.

During the boom period, 1947-1957, immigration restrictions were gradually eased to admit not only unsponsored refugees and displaced persons but ordinary immigrants from a growing number of countries. The nominal credit for banishing racism from Canada's immigration policy belongs to the Progressive Conservatives, who toppled the Grits in the federal election of 10 June 1957 after a 22-year absence from the government benches. Perhaps because of the Progressive Conservatives' reluctance to take decisive action on immigration issues, the uninfluential Citizenship and Immigration portfolio was assigned in May 1958 to Ellen Fairclough.

During her term as Minister of Citizenship and Immigration, Ellen Fairclough oversaw a steady improvement in the operation and procedures of the Immigration Service. Measured against this and her other accomplishments, however, was one of even greater significance - the long-overdue and radical reform that virtually abolished the "White Canada" immigration policy.

Canada abolishes its racist immigration policy

The reform was introduced to the public on 19 January 1962 when Ellen Fairclough tabled new regulations in the House that virtually eliminated racial discrimination as a major feature of Canada's immigration policy. Henceforth any unsponsored immigrants who had the requisite education, skill, or other qualifications were to be considered suitable for admission, irrespective of colour, race, or national origin, provided they had a specific job waiting for them in Canada, were not criminals or terrorists, and did not suffer from a disease that endangered public health.

Only one vestige of true discrimination remained and that was the provision that allowed European immigrants and immigrants from the Americas to sponsor a wider range of relatives. This clause would be removed five years later, however, in the immigration regulations of 1967. When the new regulations were implemented on 1 February 1962, Canada became the first of the three large receiving countries in international migration - the other two being the United States and Australia - to dismantle its discriminatory immigration policy.

The new regulations tabled by Fairclough in the House of Commons before she left the Department of Citizenship and Immigration were foreshadowed by John Diefenbaker's cherished Canadian Bill of Rights (1960). Since the Bill of Rights had rejected discrimination by reason of race, colour, national origin, religion, or sex, the federal government could no longer justify selecting immigrants on the basis of race or national origin. Moreover, the long-standing discriminatory provisions now seemed anachronistic and untenable in an era when provincial governments were legislating against discrimination on the basis of race, religion, and origin in such areas as employment, education, and accommodation.

The points system

By far the most significant development in immigration policy in these years, however, was the introduction of the points system, a method designed to eliminate caprice and prejudice in the selection of independent immigrants. In the points system, immigration officers assign points up to a fixed maximum in each of several categories, such as education, employment opportunities in Canada, age, the individual's personal characteristics, and degree of fluency in English or French.

The points system was incorporated into new immigration

regulations that went into effect in 1967. Other features of these regulations included the elimination of discrimination based on nationality or race from all classes of immigrants and the creation of a special provision that allowed visitors to apply for immigrant status while in Canada. Closely related to this last provision was the passage of the *Immigration Appeal Board Act* (1967), which set up a new and fully independent appeal board. Anyone who had been ordered deported could appeal to the board, no matter what his or her status was under the *Immigration Act.*

During the first four years of Pierre Trudeau's administration, from 1968 to 1972, Ministers of Manpower and Immigration came and went with unseemly frequency. Nevertheless, the Prime Minister paved the way for a dramatic and sorely needed overhaul of Canadian immigration policy when he appointed Robert Andras Minister of Manpower and Immigration in November 1972. Robert Andras was convinced that Canada would only obtain a decent *Immigration Act* when an answer was found to the basic question "Why do we have immigration to this country?"

In his quest to find answers to this fundamental question, the Minister invited the provinces and any interested organizations to submit briefs. He also commissioned a study to provide a factual background to policy issues and furnish policy options. The green paper was intended to provoke discussion, and indeed, after its tabling in the House of Commons in February 1975, it unleashed an unprecedented nation-wide debate on immigration policy. Subsequently, a Special Joint Senate House of Commons Committee was struck to stage public hearings on the controversial paper.

After holding 50 public hearings in 21 cities across Canada and reviewing more than 1,400 briefs submitted to it, the hard-working committee produced a report whose recommendations formed the basis of a new *Immigration Act.*

The Immigration Act, 1976

The *Immigration Act,* the cornerstone of present-day immigration policy, was enacted in 1976 and came into force in 1978. It broke new ground by spelling out the fundamental principles and objectives of Canadian immigration policy. Included among these are the promotion of Canada's demographic, economic, cultural, and social goals; family reunification; the fulfillment of Canada's international obligations in relation to the United Nations Convention (1951) and its 1967 Protocol relating to refugees, which Canada had signed in 1969; non-discrimination in immigration policy; and cooperation between all levels of government and the voluntary sector in the settlement of immigrants in Canadian society.

The Act recognizes four basic categories of individuals eligible for landed-immigrant status: (1) family class, which includes the immediate family and dependent children, as well as parents and grandparents over 60, or if widowed or incapable of earning a livelihood, under 60; (2) humanitarian class, which includes (a) refugees as defined in the 1951 United Nations Convention relating to refugees and (b) persecuted and displaced persons who do not qualify as refugees under the rigid UN definition but who are members of a specially designated class created by the Cabinet for humanitarian reasons; (3) independent class, which comprises applicants who apply for landed-immigrant status on their own initiative and are selected on the basis of the points system; and (4) assisted relatives, that is, more distant relatives who are sponsored by a family member in Canada and who meet some of the selection criteria of the independent class.

The 1976 *Immigration Act* received almost unanimous support from all parties in the House. The changes set in motion by the abolition of Canada's racist immigration policy and the introduction of the points system did not take long to become apparent. In 1966, almost 87 percent of Canada's immigrants had been of European origin, while only four years later 50 percent came from quite different regions of the world: the West Indies, Guyana, Haiti, Hong Kong, India, the Philippines, and Indochina.

Throughout the 1970s and 1980s, newcomers would emigrate from Africa, Asia, the Caribbean, or Latin America and they would settle in disproportionate numbers in the lower Fraser Valley (the heavily populated area extending from Hope, British Columbia, to Vancouver), the Toronto area, and the greater Montréal region. To even the casual observer, it was obvious that visible ethnic and racial minorities were becoming a significant part of Canada's social fabric. By contrast, other parts of the country, such as the four Atlantic provinces, remained virtually untouched by this immigration.

Canada's immigration policy has always had to adapt to the emerging socio-political conditions at home as well as abroad. After it removed racial and geographical discrimination from its immigration policy and belatedly signed the Geneva Convention relating to the Status of Refugees and its 1967 Protocol, refugees from outside Europe could apply for and frequently gain admission to this country.

In 1971 and 1972 Canada admitted some 228 Tibetans. Along with their fellow countrymen, these refugees had fled their homeland after China occupied it in 1959. Led by their Dalai Lama or spiritual leader, they had sought sanctuary in Nepal, but they were not welcome there.

Among the newcomers accepted from Africa in these years was a group of well-trained and highly educated Asians who had been expelled from Uganda by Idi Amin's decree of August 1972. In response to an urgent appeal from the British government, Pierre Trudeau's Liberal government decided to accept some 5,000 of these refugees.

After the violent overthrow of Salvador Allende's socialist-communist government in 1973 over 7,000 Chilean and other Latin American refugees were admitted to Canada. Chilean and non-Chilean supporters of the old regime had fled the oppression directed against them by Chile's new military ruler, General Pinochet, in the wake of the coup.

Canada was humanitarian in its response to the plight of the Vietnamese, Laotians, and Kampucheans who fled Communist regimes in the wake of Saigon's fall in 1975. In 1979 and 1980, it accepted approximately 60,000 of these refugees, most of whom had endured several days in small, leaky boats, prey to vicious pirate attacks, before ending up in squalid camps in Thailand and Malaysia. Their numbers were such that they comprised 25 percent of all the newcomers to this country between 1978 and 1981, a very high proportion given that refugees normally make up only about 10 percent of the annual flow to Canada.

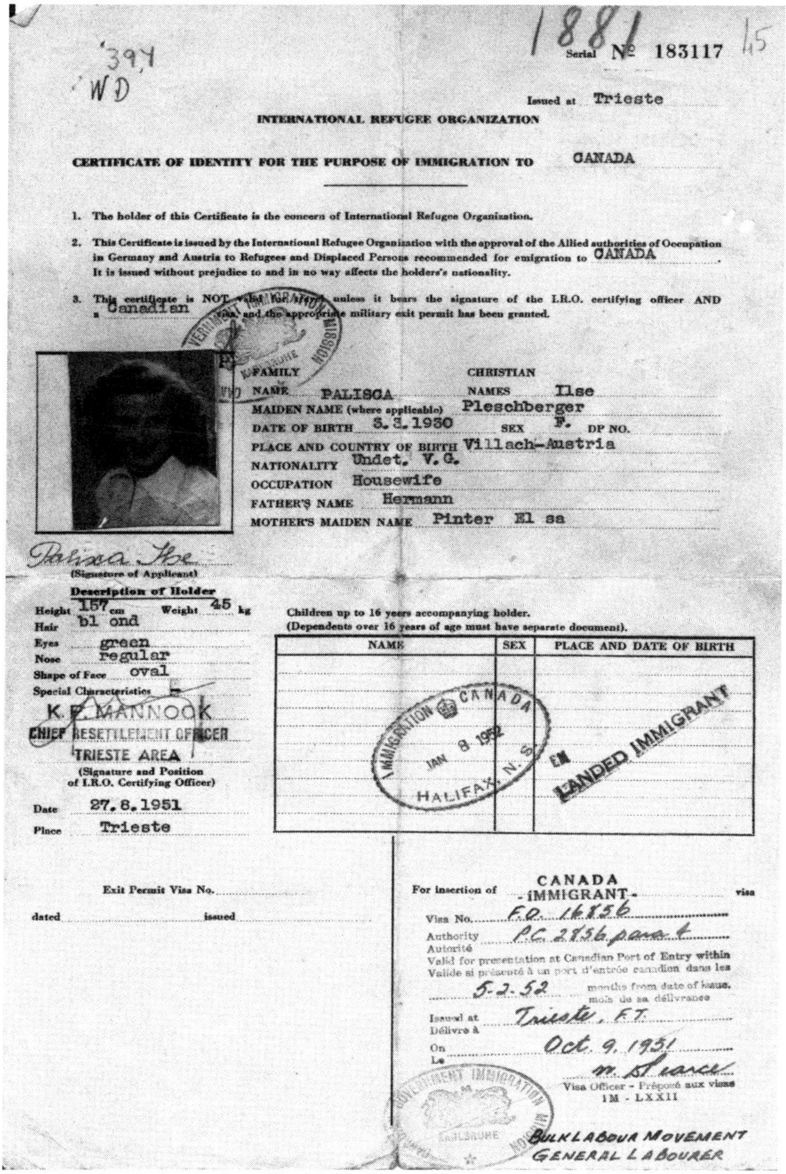

1881   Serial № 183117   45

394
WD

Issued at Trieste

INTERNATIONAL REFUGEE ORGANIZATION

CERTIFICATE OF IDENTITY FOR THE PURPOSE OF IMMIGRATION TO CANADA

1. The holder of this Certificate is the concern of International Refugee Organization.
2. This Certificate is issued by the International Refugee Organization with the approval of the Allied authorities of Occupation in Germany and Austria to Refugees and Displaced Persons recommended for emigration to CANADA. It is issued without prejudice to and in no way affects the holders's nationality.
3. This certificate is NOT valid for travel unless it bears the signature of the I.R.O. certifying officer AND a Canadian visa and the appropriate military exit permit has been granted.

FAMILY NAME PALISCA   CHRISTIAN NAMES Ilse
MAIDEN NAME (where applicable) Pleschberger
DATE OF BIRTH 3.3.1930   SEX F.   DP NO.
PLACE AND COUNTRY OF BIRTH Villach-Austria
NATIONALITY Undet. V.G.
OCCUPATION Housewife
FATHER'S NAME Hermann
MOTHER'S MAIDEN NAME Pinter El sa

Palisca Ilse
(Signature of Applicant)

Description of Holder
Height 157 cm   Weight 45 kg
Hair bl ond
Eyes green
Nose regular
Shape of Face oval
Special Characteristics

K. P. MANNOCK
CHIEF RESETTLEMENT OFFICER
TRIESTE AREA
(Signature and Position of I.R.O. Certifying Officer)

Date 27.8.1951
Place Trieste

Children up to 16 years accompanying holder.
(Dependents over 16 years of age must have separate document).

NAME	SEX	PLACE AND DATE OF BIRTH

IMMIGRATION CANADA JAN 8 1952 HALIFAX, N.S.
LANDED IMMIGRANT

Exit Permit Visa No.
dated   issued

For insertion of CANADA - IMMIGRANT - visa
Visa No. F.O. 16856
Authority / Autorité P.C. 2856 para 4
Valid for presentation at Canadian Port of Entry within / Valide si présenté à un port d'entrée canadien dans les 5-2-52 months from date of issue. / mois de sa délivrance
Issued at / Délivré à Trieste, F.T.
On / Le Oct. 9, 1951
M. Pearce
Visa Officer - Préposé aux visas
1M - LXXII

BULK LABOUR MOVEMENT
GENERAL LABOURER

Ilse Palisca has fond memories of Pier 21. The Fairsea, that brought her to Canada landed in Halifax on January 8, 1952. She is now 70 years old but has lived to see a dream come true. On July 20, 2000, forty eight years later, she travelled by train to Halifax to set foot on Pier 21 again. Courtesy: Pier 21 Society

British guest children arrive at Pier 21 in 1941. Photo: E.A. Bollinger. Courtesy: Public Archives of Nova Scotia

Immigrants walk across a ship's gangplank that connects with Pier 21 in Halifax. *Photo courtesy: Pier 21 Society*

Top: Evacuee children aboard the ship Bayano, August , 1940
Courtesy: Catherene Reid/Pier 21 Society

Right: Polish refugees
Photo courtesy: National Archives of Canada

How Canada is challenged today

War and conflict in the last couple of decades have challenged host countries like Canada, the USA, Australia and Europe to accept more refugees even as the UNHCR grapples with an ever-growing refugee crisis kicked up by the conflicts in Iraq, the former Yugoslavia, Rwanda and Africa's Great Lakes region. The series of war crises had taken the refugee count to an all-time high of 27 million in 1995 before gradually tapering off at the end of the century. But now, as the war on terrorism looms over Afghanistan, a bigger refugee crisis is on the horizon. As thousands of Afghan citizens make attempts to flee the country seeking refuge across the borders, Pakistan and Iran have sealed them.

UNHCR's founding mandate defines refugees as people who are outside their country and cannot return owing to a well-founded fear of persecution, because of their race, religion, nationality, political opinion or membership of a particular social group. However, regional instruments such as the 1969 Organization of African Unity (OAU) Refugee Convention and the 1984 Cartagena Declaration expanded that mandate to include people who have fled because of war or civil conflict.

A total of 139 countries have signed the 1951 Geneva Refugee Convention and its 1967 Protocol and recognize people as refugees based on the definitions contained in these and the regional instruments. Canada, as a party to the 1951 convention and its 1967 Protocol, has enacted relevant national legislation. At the end of 1998, it had hosted about 159,000 refugees and asylum seekers. In the same year some 24,000 people had applied for refugee status and out of the 23,200 cases decided, Canada granted refugee status to 12,880.

At the same time, Canada has been challenged lately by people-smuggling operations that have seen boat-loads of Chinese people, for example, being illegally smuggled into Canada's West coast. In February 2000, at least 25 Chinese migrants hiding aboard a freight ship that docked at Seattle, faced deportation. But the dock was full and the ship sailed off for Vancouver. Canada Customs agents found the men locked inside two canvas covered cargo containers.

Four months later, 90 Chinese migrants were deported from Canada under armed guard. They were among the almost 600 migrants that arrived off the West Coast. Almost at the same time, two Cuban stowaways had been denied stay in Canada because they had requested "economic asylum" according to immigration officials. Other sympathizers said their deportation to Cuba could put their lives at risk in a Cuban-a-la-fidel justice system. Reports in the media once again opened the debate on whether or not Canada should deport people despite knowing that the refugee seeking asylum would be subject to torture or death in his own country. But at the other end of the spectrum, Canada is also criticized for harbouring criminals as well as for making itself a conduit for these people to enter the United States. The September 11 crisis has forced Canada to introduce security strategies into its immigration plan.

Bill C-11

These and other abuses of Canadian immigration law have riveted Ottawa's attention to the need for reform of the *Immigration Act* of 1976. In the early part of this year, Elinor Caplan, Minister of Citizenship and Immigration tabled the *Immigration and Refugee Protection Act* in the House of Commons, reaffirming her commitment to be tough on criminals, while strengthening efforts to attract skilled immigrants.

The new bill incorporates a number of recent proposals from Canadians, yet maintains the core principles and provisions of Bill C-31, the immigration legislation introduced prior to last fall's general election. The Minister said the legislation reintroduces severe penalties - fines of up to $1 million and life in prison - for people smugglers and traffickers, speeds up family reunification, and maintains Canada's humanitarian tradition of providing a safe haven to people in need of protection.

The bill reintroduces key measures to strengthen the integrity of the refugee determination system. These include front-end security screening for all claimants, clearer grounds for detention, fewer appeals and opportunities for judicial review to delay the removal of serious criminals and suspension of refugee claims for people charged with serious crimes until the courts have rendered a decision. The legislation reaffirms the commitment to faster but fair decisions on refugee claims by consolidating several current steps and criteria into a single protection decision to be made by the Immigration and Refugee Board.

Furthermore, the new bill reintroduces a number of key provisions designed to expand the admission of workers with the skills that are most acutely needed in Canada. The key changes that have emerged from discussions of Bill C-31 and that were introduced include: 1. The inclusion of the definition of permanent resident in the Act. 2. Provisions within the bill that reinforce the government's commitment to gender equality and clarify that parents are members of the family class. 3. An oral appeal hearing for people facing a loss of permanent resident status for failure to maintain residency. 4. Improved safeguards for people in need of protection: unsuccessful repeat refugee claimants will be eligible for a pre-removal risk assessment (PRRA) if they return to Canada after six months (as opposed to one year). 5. Discretion for oral PRRA in exceptional circumstances. 6. Eligibility to apply for Canadian refugee travel documents for protected people whose identities have been established. 7. The requirement of a warrant to arrest refugees and permanent residents for any immigration matter. 8. The principle that children will be detained only as a last resort.

The Minister has promised supporting regulations over the coming months, which will include a strengthened overseas refugee resettlement program, an expanded family class, new selection criteria to attract more highly skilled and adaptable independent immigrants, and the creation of an "in-Canada" landing class for temporary workers, foreign students and spouses already established in Canada and wishing to stay. The expanded family class will increase the age at which a dependent child can be sponsored from under 19 to under 22 and allow spouses and children to apply for permanent residence from within Canada. The Minister also expressed willingness to pursue discussions with the provinces over additional ways to expand the family class. The new legislation will replace the current *Immigration Act*, which was first passed in 1976 and which has been amended more than 30 times.

Refugees and Canada

Refugees overseas, who have not yet found a permanent home can be resettled in Canada. The Canadian government, every year, determines a specified quota of refugees for resettlement. In addition, a private group (an organization, such as a church, or a group of individuals) can resettle a refugee or a refugee family, subject to the government approving the sponsorship.

Of course, refugees are interviewed and processed overseas by Canadian visa officers before being resettled. This process is sometimes long drawn.

On the other hand, refugees who have not been selected overseas can claim Canada's protection at a border point or from within Canada. Their claim will be reviewed for eligibility, where the concerns are whether or not the individual has already been recognized as a refugee by another country or if the person raises serious criminality or security concerns. If the claim is found to be eligible, it is referred to the Immigration and Refugee Board (IRB), an independent quasi-judicial tribunal, which hears the claim. There is very limited legal recourse in the event of a negative decision.

Settlement and integration of refugees and immigrants in Canada

There are several community agencies across the country which assist refugees and immigrants in the process of adaptation – whether that be orientation, training in English or French language skills or finding employment. Indeed, even the special needs of many refugees who have survived torture are addressed.

Nonetheless advocacy groups have expressed reservations about Canada's treatment of refugees. The Canadian Council for Refugees (CCR), for example, has criticized the fact that the legislation does not allow a refugee claimant who is determined not to be a refugee to appeal the decision on its merits, even if new information is available supporting the claim. The only form of review is by application to the Federal Court, for which permission must be granted. The Federal Court can only overturn the decision if there are serious legal errors.

Furthermore, legal aid coverage for refugee claims varies from province to province, but in many parts of the country it is either minimal or non-existent. This means that many refugee claimants must present their case for refugee status with poor legal representation, or none at all.

Since 1993 the law has required refugees recognized in Canada to proffer identity documents before they can be landed. The law has been criticized for being unrealistic. The fact is that many refugees are often in a legal limbo – during Somalia's civil war, for example, a Somalian refugee would not be able to obtain an identity document because there was no government to issue one.

On the other hand, women are disproportionately affected because in many societies women have limited access to identity documents.

Lee Cohen, whose law practice in Halifax is dedicated to immigration and human rights, says Canada must honour its international commitments to provide a safe haven for those escaping persecution. Much of Cohen's work takes place at the Immigration and Refugee Board (IRB). He points to the fact that IRB judges are political appointees, many who do not clearly perceive what persecution is in other parts of the world. Cohen believes it takes a sophisticated thinker to realize that a refugee has had to lie in order to live. It's obvious that religious, cultural and political repression in other parts of the world do not allow a victim to report, say, a rape incident.

Refugees out of Burundi in Africa

According to the 1951 Convention relating to the Status of Refugees, a refugee is an individual who is outside his or her country, who has a well-founded fear of being persecuted for reasons of race, religion, nationality, membership of a particular social group or political opinion, and whom the state is unwilling or unable to protect. The definition, according to CCR, does not mention gender and has traditionally tended to be interpreted in a way that does not take account of women's experiences of persecution.

It's just as well that in 1993 Canada became the first country to introduce a legislative framework on refugee women claimants fleeing gender-related persecution. The Beijing Conference on Women in 1995 recognized problems connected with violence against women and called for action against it. The Platform for Action calls for consideration to be given to recognizing as refugees, women whose claim to refugee status is based on a well-founded fear of persecution "including persecution through sexual violence or other gender-related persecution".

Emigration out of Africa

Emigration out of Africa

During the famines that swept across Africa in 1985 some 35 million Africans went hungry and perhaps a third of that figure abandoned their homes in search of food and water.

Africa may have chronic problems with feeding itself but economic deprivation is not Africa's only problem – its misery is made worse by the inevitable cycle of unemployment, migration to towns, congested cities and above all, civil strife, repression and human rights abuses. What compounds the problem is that Africa lacks leadership. Furthermore, the continent's wealth is concentrated among ten per cent of its people.

Not even a famine that threatened millions in Ethiopia satiated the hunger for blood as it went to war with its

Young Kenyan kicks the bottle to begin a new life

Jaoko Odinga, the drunk whom the RCMP once picked up on a street in Halifax when he had crashed his bicycle on a lamp post is the grandson of independent Kenya's first Vice president Oginga Odinga.

Odinga was born in Moscow to African parents. In the Cold War era, Russia had been wooing students from the developing world and had offered Kenyans the scholarships to study in Moscow. Odinga's parents took the offer – his father did a doctorate in Economics

Jaoko Odinga

and his mother got a medical degree. But when it was time for Odinga to go to school, the family moved back to Kenya and the boy later travelled to Zimbabwe when Kenya threw out the British curricula from its schools and Africanized the education system.

His grandfather Oginga Odinga served as Kenya's Vice President in Jomo Kenyatta's *neighbour Eritrea.*

In Sierra Leone, the nightmare of terror, mutilation of children, the skinning of opponents went unabated for eight years before rebel leader Foday Sankoh was captured.

In Somalia, the trauma of civil war drove its people to neighbouring Kenya for refuge. Hadil Hasan, who came to Canada as a refugee recalls : "The war was traumatic for all of us. Every couple of steps along the way to the Kenyan border we saw blood and death, children maimed, people skinned alive.

Hasan who was made to witness her husband's assassination says she wonders if those sights of horror, shall ever be erased from her memory or if her life, shall at all, restore some meaning to her existence.

When Idi Amin came to power in Uganda and told citizens of Indian heritage to leave his country, the crisis saw 80,000

government in 1963. But in rough times, he fell from Kenyatta's favour, was accused of being communist and when he led the campaign for a multi-party democracy in Kenya, Kenyatta banned all opposition parties and jailed Odinga's grandfather. It was only 24 years later in 1991 when Daniel Arap Moi conceded to multiparty opposition. Odinga's father is now a Member of Parliament, in opposition to Moi's government.

His was a wealthy family. But wealth was not what he was going after apparently. "I wanted to set my own goals and take my own paths," he says. So he made tracks to Canada in 1992 and began his studies at Saint Mary's University.

"Life in Canada, upon coming to Halifax, was one big party," Odinga recalls. "I had my first drink at 13. I realized drinking was something I was good at. I drank everybody under the table. Of course, I also realized giving up drinks was very easy. I did it several times," he says, laughing heartily. Odinga does not look back in anger at those days when alcohol took him down the wrong road – quite literally.

On Christmas day, for example, he walked through a glass door and woke up in hospital. On graduation day, he crashed against a lamp post while on a bicycle and was shown his way home by the RCMP. "I realized I was working only to drink. By the time my pay cheque came in, I had borrowed more than what it was worth."

He says he was seeing a faithful girl. "She lived with my blackouts and all my problems. Those four years were hell. My life was going down a tube. I was destroying every bit of me – including the trading business I had set up in 1998 – bringing in merchandise shipments from Zimbabwe."

They say only the man on the highest mountain knows what it is to be in the lowest valley. Odinga identifies with that feeling. He *people fleeing the country in days. "It became almost impossible to live in Uganda at the time," recalls Jerry Braganza who fled Uganda and was granted refugee status in Canada: "Homes were being blown up and jobs were "africanized".*

When the United Nations and the Organization of African Unity (OAU) called for Eritrea's federation with Ethiopia in 1952, Eritreans took their political destinies in their hands and in 1961 began what was to become a 30-year civil war for self-determination. The resistance years were fraught with suspicion of political dissidence, fear of torture and the stifling of thought and expression. Eritreans in key positions were transferred to Addis in Ethiopia. The other Eritreans suspected to be potential accomplices with the Eritrean resistance movement were despatched to the hinterland. The Red Terror unleashed by Ethiopia from 1975

remembers the feeling that drinking was isolating him. " I was once very confident when I drank, now I began to feel ashamed," he says. "I was so broke one day, I did the shameful thing: I pinched my girlfriend's credit card and she caught me in the act. I realized that if I could stoop so low, it meant I had to kick the bottle."

The Alcoholics Anonymous is that light at the end of the tunnel for drunks and just as well Odinga was being drawn to it by the girl he was seeing. "Once I had thought the AA was for bums. Now I knew it was for me," he says. "I was drunk at the first AA meeting. But when I heard people confess to the shameful things they did as drunks, I found a sense of hope. From then on Odinga was steering his life in another direction. Like most alcoholics, he was swearing the AA motto: One day at a time. "Now I see serenity in sobriety and I like the feeling," he admits.

While, all along Odinga has been wanting to do something with an e-commerce based business, he has finally got down to marketing batik paintings from Tanzania's most famous painters. The business is picking up speed. "The paintings sell for a song. You can see curiosity and excitement among Canadians when they behold African batik paintings at such prices.

But in the summer of 2002 Odinga is about to embark on something more exciting and by far nobler. He is teaming up with the Southern African Association of Nova Scotia (SANS) to stage the Inter.Continental Carnival Extravaganza (ICCE). This will include cultural parades down Gottingen street, accompanied by popular bands as well as workshops on carnival costumes and native or Gaelic traditions."

to 1990 reportedly killed 100,000 people. The secret service agency "Kebele" was allegedly tracking down rebels and executing them in their units, forcing an exodus of refugees.

In Sudan, the scourge of the slave trade has been revived in the midst of civil war. Sudan's problems are driven by both ethnic strife and religious bigotry. The northern Sudanese who have traditionally wrested power comprise Muslim Arab and Middle Eastern peoples while the southern population is made up of Black African Christians. When in 1983, Sudan's ruler Jaffar Numeiri, revoked autonomy covenants and split the south into three regions, making them the Central Administrative Region, civil strife broke out and its repressed people fled to neighbouring countries for safety.

Nigeria's

Ugandan flees Idi Amin's terror and sets up business in Canada

Jerry Braganza suffered Idi Amin's wrath when he ordered his country's Asian community to get the hell out of Uganda. The former Ugandan dictator wrested power from Milton Obote in a bloody revolution in 1971 and Braganza even remembers the horrific tribal violence that was unleashed across northern Uganda at the time.

Jerry Braganza

Amin, determined to transfer the economic domination of the Indian business community to his own African people gave the Asian community three months to pack up and get out.

A third generation Indian born in Entebbe, Braganza says the crisis created some 80,000 Indian refugees, some scurrying back to India others to Britain. "It became almost impossible to live in Uganda. Houses were being blown up and jobs were *africanized*, he says.

civil war between 1966 and 1970 drove thousands of its countrymen into neighbouring Ghana.

Levi Ezurike, a financial analyst of Nigerian heritage says he had seen it coming and had immigrated to Ghana sometime earlier. But as he observes today, the power struggles in Africa driven by greed and the exploitation of ethnic loyalties have impoverished the continent, creating armies of refugees. Levi had to leave Ghana some years later for the same reasons. The overthrow of Kwami Nkruma changed the political atmosphere and the policies of the new military government were geared against foreigners.

In South Africa during the apartheid years, it was commonplace to hear bombs go off in school. The colour bar, overall, meant that neighbourhoods and schools were segregated on the basis of race, while regardless of skills, opportunity was limited.

Braganza's parents decided to leave for India, but what did he know of India. "Fortunately I held a British passport, so I chose, instead, to move to Britain. I had lived a life of luxury in Uganda," he admits. "Then overnight, I became a stateless refugee."

Amin's government had asked banks to freeze the accounts of all Indians to intensify the exodus and so the young man was left with an air ticket and $100, a pair of jeans and a T-shirt.

He says he vividly remembers the drive to Entebbe airport. "It was scary. There were road blocks everywhere. The military was stopping people, grabbing jewellery and being brutal with the people fleeing. All of them were empowered to shoot."

In England, Braganza lived in a refugee camp while his visa to Canada was being processed. He says he and other fellow refugees were given two Sterling Pounds per day "which was more than enough for a bottle of beer." His landed immigrant visa to Canada came in four months later and in a week's time, he picked up a job at Maritime Marlin in Halifax. A little later he got married to Rita who, although raised in Mombasa, lived in Uganda at the time and had to flee.

"Of course the early days in Canada were fraught with problems - loneliness, being the biggest of all.

Braganza is no stranger to Canada today. Ten years after working with several travelling agencies, he set up Aeroworld Travels in Halifax. The company boasts a whopping $3.5 million turnover in tickets, holidays and hotel rooms sold per year. He says his success comes from having a good crop of travel agents .

"Today there are problems in the travel industry. But we've made it through tough times before. We'll pull through this," he says.

South Africa, at the time, was exporting apartheid to Namibia. Namibian refugees in Canada say white colonies were barred to the blacks after sundown. The Namibian students who protested - and especially those from left-wing political parties fighting the South African regime were arrested and jailed. The hostile environment forced young Namibians to flee to Botswana and from there to other refugee hosting countries.

Canada has also welcomed refugees from Angola, where after independence from Portugal, severe hostilities had broken out between UNITA rebels and the government.

Somalian hopes Canada will erase horror memories

Hadil Hassan who was in the deadly midst of it all during the civil war in Somalia is hoping that life in Canada shall someday erase those memories.

Hadil's child was nine days old when a gang of looters broke into her house and seized her husband. "They wanted all our money and my jewellery," she says. "I said I would give anything for my husband's life. But they shot him in the head, buried him in the backyard and left."

A couple of days later, Hadil's father's house was blown up and as the bloody civil war penetrated the neighbouring villages, Hadil's family chose to flee. Her husband's people fled to Kenya and Hadil's family began the long journey across the border to Ethiopia.

"The war was traumatic," Hadil says. "Every couple of steps along the way we saw blood and death, children maimed ."

The journey to Ethiopia took a couple of months. Hadil even lost her mother along the way , thankfully for only a couple of days. In Ethiopia, they lived on wheat brought to the refugee camps by the Red Cross.

But war also has a way of tearing people apart. So when a couple of years later, her father proposed that she marry her husband's brother, she travelled to Kenya with him, leaving her son behind with her mother.

Hadil's second husband was a translator at the Canadian mission in Kenya and that obviously made the Canadian connection. The Hassans came to Canada two years ago. But the trials were far from over.

When Hadil's father returned home to Somalia with her son, he was assasinated. The boy's early years were a witness to the ugliness of Somalia's civil war.

But Hadil knows deep inside her that a reunion with her son in Canada will bring a new dawn.

Nigerian wrestler says Canadians truly appreciate diversity

Daniel Igali, is not sure if immigrating can be compared to changing religions – but he surely knows that it takes great courage to get up and go. "When I left my home in Nigeria at the age of 20, I had to take some tough decisions – of leaving behind everything I had achieved by then – my education, friends and family.

Igali arrived in Canada with the Nigerian contingent for the Commonwealth games. "My decision to stay was not predetermined. That decision was made on Canadian soil," he says. "Of course what guided my decision to stay was the worsening political situation in Nigeria and my commitment to combine education and sports.

He says, he does have the urge to go back because "I have close and emotional ties with my parents and siblings alike. Thankfully, my sponsors, General Mills (Cheerios) have made it possible for me to travel to Nigeria twice a year. That gives me a measure of peace that I need to concentrate on my sport.

Igali believes he has been lucky to have met people in Canada who made his settlement process very easy. "I have experienced what the transition from a collectivist to an individualistic society entails, but I have weathered it. It's important to take the good from both cultures and making a go of it."

His finest moment in sport flashed when he won the World Championship title in freestyle wrestling in Ankara in 1999. "It was the first time a Canadian had done it. It was also the first time that someone of African descent had achieved this," he says. "It was quite a feat."

Igali is an Olympic Gold Medallist

But while he is proud of his world championship title, Igali says, it was the winning of the Olympic Gold Medal that brought him recognition.

The young wrestler graduated from Simon Fraser University with a degree in Criminology. That combined to crown his achievements in sport.

What does Igali feel about Canada's diversity? Is it truly a multicultural society? "Canada," he says, "is the best country in the world. In my opinion, Canadians truly appreciate a multicultural society. Of course, one might run into a few ignorant people, sometimes, who believe they own Canada. But that is only a rarity and an exception."

Eritrean banker flees country while on a pilgrimage

In peace times, they say, you prepare for war. It's just as well that Ethiopia and Eritrea have once again talked peace after a recent war that devastated Eritrea, probably the poorest nation in the world.

The aftermath of war, anyway, shows you not just the stench of death or the trails of destruction, but a people and a mindset torn apart.

Beku Fesshaye was a senior banker in Eritrea. But as he recalls today, the resistance years from 1961 to 1991 after Eritrea's "imposed federation" with Ethiopia, were fraught with suspicion of political dissidence, fear of torture and the stifling of expression.

In 1978, Fesshaye, along with other Eritreans in key positions, was transferred to Addis in Ethiopia. The other Eritreans suspected to be potential accomplices with the Eritrean resistance movement were despatched to the hinterland.

Feshaye says the "Red Terror" that Ethiopia unleashed from 1975 to 1990 saw at least 100,000 people killed. He says the secret service agency "Kebele" tracked down rebels and executed them in their units. "I knew I was being watched. I was accused of being sympathetic to the Eritrean Liberation Front. I was interrogated by security agents and threatened to be shot," he says.

The United Nations and the Organization of African Unity (OAU) have been accused of being mindless of the geographical needs in the Horn of Africa for calling for Eritrea's federation with Ethiopia in 1952. The UN decision forced Eritreans to take their political destinies in their hands and in 1961 began what was to become a 30-year civil war for self-determination.

Fesshaye says that by 1986 Eritreans brought the rebellion to Ethiopia. They made a tacit alliance with the neighbouring province of Tibrail to exploit Ethiopia's vulnerability to a breakdown on ethnic grounds.

"But when the war was brought to Addis in 1990, I had to escape," says Fesshaye, who worked for the Commercial Bank of Ethiopia at the time and where his movements were watched very closely.

He had three options: one was a border crossing. But he chose not to take that one. When his sister fled across the border to Sudan, she was conscripted by force and later killed in action.

So Fesshaye joined a pilgrimage organization that was making travel arrangements for Christians to leave for Fatima, Lourdes and the Holy Lands. The pilgrimage brought him to Italy and opened some windows on the world. He had left behind his wife and children, living in fear of their safety during the four years of separation after his flight out of Eritrea.

In those four years he travelled from Italy to the US and from there into Canada through the Peace Bridge in Ontario.

But as some newcomers to Canada say, fleeing to Canada does not necessarily open the gates to heaven. Fesshaye was granted refugee status after a year of tribunal hearings. "There was evidence of preferential treatment accorded to refugees from Europe," he says.

In the seven years that he has been in Canada, he has held junior positions at the data centre of TD Bank, CIBC and ScotiaBank in Toronto. "But I realized that a career as a banker was over for me. My colour and my accent were barriers. You may see a couple of black or brown faces at the front desks of banks, but inside it's all white. You begin to wonder if you are there by accident," he says.

"Racism is a system. It's not about a man telling you: I hate you. The job market and the workplace are evidence of systemic racism."

Of course, he backs down to admit that Canada is a free country with a sense of justice. "If you are exceptional in the profession, the system accepts you and colour is tucked under the carpet."

Beku Fesshaye

So what does the future hold for Fesshaye. "No future for myself," he says. "There are barriers. After seven years of visiting the local Church for Holy Mass on Sundays, we find that we know nobody, although the Church is a community of people. There are other Africans who feel like me."

But he knows there could be a future for his children. "They have aspirations. If they surmount the barriers, they will accomplish something," he says with a sense of hope.

Christian mission connects Sudanese with his family

The Sudan's problems did not end when it broke itself free from Britain in January 1956. An uprising among rival groups was brewing shortly before independence which has since mired this African nation of 30 million people in civil strife.

But although Sudan still grapples with its problems almost five decades later, Alex Atiol has broken free from it and is working to surmount the new challenges that life in Canada presents to newcomers like him.

Atiol, who works with the Metropolitan Immigrant Settlement Association (MISA) in Halifax, says he has had to leave a plum job with the British organization ODA (Overseas Development Agency) when Sudan's rebel army captured the town Yei in 1990.

Sudan's problems are driven by both ethnic strife and religious bigotry. The northern Sudanese who have traditionally wrested power comprise Muslim Arab and Middle Eastern peoples while the southern population is made up of Black African Christians.

In 1972, Sudan was within grasp of peace when the government in the North granted the south autonomy. But as Atiol explains this tryst with peace was short-lived. In 1983, Jaffar Numeiri, Sudan's then ruler broke the peace, revoking autonomy covenants and split the south into three regions,

Alex Atiol

making them the Central Administrative Region. Consequently, civil strife tore across The Sudan once again.

Atiol and his family, along with thousands of civilians left the rebel stronghold Yei when it was captured from government forces and fled for safety to Kaya, a town bordering Uganda. He settled there for a year in a camp for internally displaced civilians, braving hardship and relying on food supplies from UN relief agencies.

In the heat of that war, Atiol says, the civilian population was extremely vulnerable to the crossfire, air raids and bombardment by government forces. But a decree by the leader of the SPLA at the time called for conscription of young men and shortly afterwards he began work as a bookkeeper, collecting taxes for the SPLA in rebel-captured towns. Conscription involved training in battle. But Atiol did not want that. Nor did he want to be entrenched in the dirty business of war – that might never be won and never end.

He worked out a secret plan to evict himself from Kaya. He told the SPLA he was leaving family behind to see his mother in Chickadum and that he would return to reunite with his family. Although Atiol could leave Kaya, "things did not work out in Chickadum," he says. The flight of a refugee, sometimes, appears never to end. He ultimately joined several other fleeing Africans on a 100-kilometre trek on foot to a border town in Kenya, where he declared himself a refugee in 1992.

He spent the next couple of years working towards reuniting with his family, a feat that a Christian mission in Uganda ultimately accomplished for him, connecting with its mission in Kaya to extricate the family out of there.

With war out of the way, Atiol contacted Windle trust – a charitable organization that works with World University Services of Canada (WUSC). The mission of Windle Trust is to assist refugee students under 29 that want to study in Canada and who meet the basic qualifying criteria with education and skills.

It happened quickly. Atiol was admitted to Dalhousie university which ultimately brought him to Canada. WUSC sponsored his first year studies and settlement expenses. He majored in economics.

Of course, Atiol's job at the Metropolitan Immigrant Settlement Association (MISA) has little to do with bookkeeping or economics. But isn't that a familiar refrain you hear from newcomers. There is an interesting statistic that explains Alex's predicament: Citizenship and Immigration Canada reports that between 1991 and 1994, for example, 10,279 immigrants arrived in Canada listing civil, mechanical, chemical or electrical engineering as their intended occupation. By April 1996, according to Statistics Canada, only 5,770 or 46 per cent of those immigrants were practising these professions.

But Atiol is going to focus on making things better, not bigger. "I plan to go back to school and compete. But for now, I have a family to raise," he says.

Guinean student wins case in Human Rights court

Bashir Jallow's father was in the diamond trade when he moved the family from Sierra Leone to Guinea. But when communist politicians took power in Guinea, his father's wealth was being closely watched.

Guinea was among the first African states to gain independence in 1958. The communist regime which seized power then ruled until 1984 when intellectuals and businessmen were seen as threats.

"Whereas I once had a closed mind to other faiths, I now see the need to understand other people. Now I feel I should never have felt like I did not belong in Canada."

"Every time government forces came looking to arrest my father and he was away, my mother would be dragged to jail," says Jallow. "This went on until, we were finally alerted of soldiers coming to arrest us one night. I was only three years old. My father abandoned all his wealth and possessions and drove across the border into Sierra Leone and later travelled to Senegal."

Jallow went to school in Senegal, while his father was starting out all over again. It was difficult for the Jallows. But when the communist president Sekutere died and the military took power, Guinea was liberalized and former citizens returned home, including the Jallows.

He came to Canada for his tertiary education and was first admitted to Langara College in British Columbia. "It was difficult, at first," he says. "It's not just the language barrier, I speak about. Africans coming to Canada have to learn how to make the transition from a collectivist society to an individualistic society. These concepts are a world apart."

In British Columbia, Jallow worked for 18 months with a company that he finally took to the Small Claims Court and to the Human Rights Commission and won his case. "In all of those 18 months I felt discriminated against. I was finally fired on charges that I broke company policy," he says.

Jallow says this was trumped up. "The company alleged that I had provided discounts to friends – this was against company rules," he says. "But the evidence I provided won me the case. I was not on duty the day I was supposed to have given my friends official discounts."

What does discrimination mean to Jallow? "When people treat you like you don't have a brain, it makes life difficult for you," he says.

But Canada is doing him a lot of good as well. Currently doing his Bachelor of Commerce degree at Dalhousie University, he says, he has broadened his thinking threshold. "Whereas I once had a closed mind to other faiths, I now see the need to understand other people. Now I feel I should never have felt like I did not belong in Canada."

Quoting French novelist Jacques Rousseau, Jallow says: "I think man's problems began with a greed for land. On the other hand, I believe all of us have descended from Adam and therefore should not see ourselves as being different."

South African says her life was touched by apartheid since birth

Debra Barrath's thesis, done for her Masters at the Dalhousie School of Nursing in Halifax, explores the experience of mothers from the former Yugoslavia, who were granted asylum in Canada following the war.

The thesis documents the trauma of women and children caught in the ugliness of war: the pre-war stress, the dilemma about whether to evacuate, physical deprivation, the lack of food or money – and all this in the midst of a saga of injury, death and destruction.

Barrath's own life experiences in Durban, where she grew up, gives her a lead in this research assignment because it enables her to empathize with the people mired in hardship. She was raised during the years of the emergency in South Africa and experienced probably all kinds of apartheid.

"We had bomb scares in our school and heard and saw the effects of bombs going off in our city," she says. "I've been forbidden entry into white washrooms and the color bar, overall, meant that our neighborhoods and our schools were segregated on the basis of race, while regardless of our skills, opportunity was limited."

Barrath says her life was touched by apartheid since birth and that she grew up conscious of shame being attached to the fact of being colored or of mixed race. This, she says, was exemplified in one of those school idioms: "As drunk as a colored school teacher."

South Africa's race-based society may not have encouraged social integration but her studies at the university made it possible to discreetly meet with ANC (African National Congress) people at the

Debra with her husband Donald MacLaughlin *Photo: Benno Ganz*

time.

The media stories, at the time, were hype, she says. "The kind of strength I saw in the South African people I know makes me believe South Africa has a chance. Today's South Africa, once called the gunshot capital of the world, has the potential to become a leader in Africa and bring about social justice across the continent. Africans realize South Africa knows what it is talking about, because it has suffered hardship."

Barrath, who came to Canada to do her Masters in Nursing, is not burdened by the language barriers to integration as some immigrants to Canada are, but she speaks of a culture shock that's not quite the stereotype.

"The social rules of interaction, the attitude to authority, respect and individualism are unto their own in Canada," she says. "Having said that, one is not quite sure about the expectations – all of which result in isolation, loneliness and decreased opportunities."

Barrath says immigrants want opportunities to become independent.

"It takes roughly ten years for an immigrant to become established. We need to create the mechanisms to provide tangible support and shorten that timeframe," she says.

"It's in the interest of the economy to change these conditions. In alleviating poverty among newcomers, you maximize opportunities for all Canadians."

Nigerian blames power hungry for Africa's problems

Nigeria's civil war between 1966 and 1970 drove thousands of its countrymen into neighbouring Ghana. Levi Ezurike, who saw it coming, had immigrated to Ghana sometime earlier.

But as he observes today, the power struggles in Africa driven by greed and the exploitation of ethnic loyalties have impoverished the continent, creating armies of refugees that have been fleeing violence and repression. Levi had to leave Ghana some years later for the same reasons. The overthrow of Kwami Nkruma changed the political atmosphere in Ghana dramatically, he says, and the policies of the new military government were geared against foreigners.

Levi Eziruke

When hostilities against Nigerians erupted, Levi's relatives took the long road home, while he chose instead to take the flight to the United States after Bishops College in Houston granted him admissions.

However, en route, on a stopover in Copenhagen, Levi changed his mind, having run into a Canadian. He instead took a flight to Toronto.

Levi settled down in London, Ontario, where he studied and worked his way up until his job brought him to Nova Scotia.

He studied Public Administration at Dalhousie and currently serves as a Financial Officer with the Department of Fisheries and Oceans.

He says that while all Africans identify with the Black nation, the problems of black immigrants are unto their own. Turmoil on the African continent today is forcing an exodus of people into Canada and there is, therefore, the need for a settlement catalyst.

In the Spring of 1998, Levi and a few other Africans resuscitated the defunct African-Canadian Association of Nova Scotia and formed the African Immigrants Society, an organization that's in touch with about a thousand African immigrants, typically from Somalia, Sudan, Ghana, Nigeria, Ethiopia and Eritrea. The Society is helping fellow African immigrants to settle down culturally and socially.

"Our mandate is to assist in settlement, become a voice and spokesman for African immigrants and promote heritage through a resource centre on African affairs," Levi says. He's currently working on a resource project that will provide links on a website to major newspapers in Africa. "That will enable newcomers to touch base with home."

"Africa lacks leadership. That is precisely because of the greed of the power hungry. The continent's wealth is concentrated among ten per cent of the people."

Looking back and contemplating, Levi believes that although within nations the stakes may be different, the problems are, nonetheless, the same. "Africa lacks leadership. That is precisely because of the greed of the power hungry. The continent's wealth is concentrated among ten per cent of the people." He agrees that perhaps illiteracy compounds the problem. "Nigeria's elections were not fought on pragmatic grounds, it was fought on the basis of ethnic loyalties and the illiterate masses thus voted on the wrong side."

At home in Canada, he says, the problems are different. "I think newcomers need help because visible diversity is an additional piece of baggage to carry. Canada is a great nation....but if you don't look like them, they don't see you for what you're worth. I've been in those shoes before." Of course Levi understands the chemistry problems of integrating. It happens everywhere in the world. In all societies people want homogeneity – rather than diversity.

Levi's remarks tend to echo Douglas Fisher's observations made in the *Toronto Sun* sometime ago: "How can we sustain some unity of purpose and a sense of a whole community if we project a league of national cultures within one framework. You and me and our children have enough to do with the basic problem of the French and English duality, without enshrining the whole world's diversity within our history and borders."

Emigration out of Asia-Pacific

Emigration out of Asia Pacific

The reports of Viking voyages around AD 1000 are a divergence from the emphasis on French and British explorers in Canadian history. The Germans, Italians, Portuguese, the Slavs and Greeks and even the Chinese feature in exploration reports. The Chinese tell tales of Buddhist monks who sailed from China on rafts and went ashore in AD 458 establishing settlements in Vancouver in 499. Nonetheless, the Chinese first appear only in the 1901 census data.

The late nineteenth century marked a particularly low point in China's two thousand years of recorded history. Social chaos and the terror of warlords dominated the last decade of the nineteenth century when large-scale emigration from

Chinese doctor delivers baby the night he arrives in Canada

Ten years ago Dr. Oscar Wong travelled to Kingston from his home in Halifax. Kingston was the Ontario city that beckoned him when he first came to Canada, leaving his home in Hong Kong in the late Fifties. The cityscape naturally evoked a surge of nostalgia even as a ravenous mood saw him hurrying to a Chinese restaurant. The Chinese waitress who seated him at a table made light conversation.

It's only a rare occurrence when you stumble into a cousin in a faraway land somewhere at a bar and you say: "fancy meeting you here." The Chinese waitress served up a sumptuous meal and told him the story of her life. When she had finished her tale, and he was done with his meal, Wong rose to leave, nodding with some nostalgia.

Early Chinese immigration into Canada was marked by disfranchisement and discriminatory laws – all of which primed the movement to repeal the Chinese Exclusion Act of 1923

Wong remembers. It was Canada Day 1958 when he flew to Toronto International Airport from Hong Kong as a young man. He rode on a bus a few hours later to the Kingston General Hospital, where he was on call, by default, for the Obstetrics department that night. The administration was little aware that he was arriving from Hong Kong and not on a domestic flight. A bemused new visitor to Canada, Wong could have lost his wits about him. "But I laughed heartily," he says.

"I lost no time. I hurried to the Operating

China into the US and Canada first occurred.

Widespread opium addiction and severe hardships brought about by rapid population growth forced thousands to migrate to cities. In tandem, there was the exciting discovery of gold in California. These, indeed, were the circumstances that spawned the migration of the early Chinese into America.

In Canada, until the late nineteenth century, settlement of the West was slow. Not until Confederation and the building of the Canadian Pacific Railway did the pace of settlement accelerate and the population begin to diversify.

Although, Clifford Sifton, the Minister of Interior in Wilfrid Laurier's government in 1896 disapproved of the immigration of Asians and subsequently introduced discriminatory legislation, the Chinese on the West

Dr. Oscar Wong in the Eastern Arctic

Theatre. On that first night of my arrival, I delivered a Chinese baby. The waitress who served up that sumptuous meal to me was the one."

Wong says he left mainland China in 1953 when "many were leaving China at the time". That, of course, was long after the first Chinese were drawn to the United States by the exciting discovery of gold in California and to work on the Canadian Pacific Railway in 1880s.

Wong's arrival was also long before 1971, when Canada's multiculturalism policy,

Coast continued to increase.

Indeed, on account of pressure from anti-Asian groups, the Charter granted to the Grand Trunk Pacific Railway forbade hiring Chinese for construction work.

Although by 1921 there were about 40,000 Chinese in Canada, they were, by far, kept out of the mainstream of life in Canada – segregated schools isolated them and the notorious legislation including the Chinese Exclusion Act of 1923 and the Head Tax limited their settlement.

Under the Willow Tree, a documentary produced by Canada's National Film Board, poignantly tells the story of the early life of the Chinese in Canada through the mouths of their grandchildren and depicts the hardship of settlement. The documentary is an insight into Chinese custom and value systems.

Jean Lumb in Toronto, whose father came to work in the

prompted by the nationwide response to hearings of the Royal Commission on Bilingualism and Biculturalism opened the floodgates to the rising tide of immigration from Asia.

In 1961, he became the first Chinese doctor to volunteer as a medical officer in MS Labrador in the giddying heights of the Eastern Arctic

In Halifax, Wong began a medical career as an Intern at the Victoria General Hospital, but later on went on to do cardiac research at Queen's University and more lately research in Radiation Oncology, finishing his doctorate as a Fellow of the Royal College of Physicians and Surgeons of Canada.

But those were not the only heights, Wong had aspired to reach. In 1961, he became the first Chinese doctor to volunteer as a medical officer in MS Labrador in the giddying heights of the Eastern Arctic where he spent four months. A few years ago he hung up his boots after a 26-year stint at Victoria General.

Wong is among the 5000 or more Chinese residents of Nova Scotia. He is a past-President of the Chinese Society of Nova Scotia and over two terms has given the Chinese community a place in mainstream society .

"I think we need to enhance cross-cultural understanding and encourage the Chinese to make a greater economic contribution to Nova Scotia," he says. He has held the office of President of the Nova Scotia Cancer Foundation and has sat on the Workers Compensation Board. Wong was also the Commissioner at the Human Rights Commission for four years and has served on the Atomic Energy Control Board of Canada.

coal mines in Canada says that her mother delivered babies so often that she was never sure when she was in a family way. "Our father would say that he was going down to the railway tracks to pick up a baby."

Hazel Chong in Vancouver, whose grandmother's husband came to work for the Canadian Pacific Railway as a labourer says her mother always managed to deliver her children in the wee hours of the morning so that she would not fail to serve the family their morning cereal as usual.

Chinese men, other than merchants, missionaries or diplomats were unwelcome in Canada. The head tax by 1904 was about $500. So few, if any, could bring their wives to live with them.

Mabel Nipp of Victoria, says that Chinese merchants at the time would bring poor Chinese girls, on the pretext of they being adopted daughters, to work as their maids

Vietnamese refugee says a seed will always belong to its roots

Amid a crossfire of gunshots, Jeffrey Nguyen grabbed hold of the boat on which eighty five Vietnamese were fleeing. Only eleven years of age in 1978, he sailed offshore not even knowing where he was headed. He was on the ocean for six days. On the seventh day, the boat's crew was warned of a storm. It was to hit the ocean in less than ten hours causing the boat to capsize. Nguyen could have perished as well– but it was not to be. A Libyan ship transporting oil to Japan rescued the boat and brought it to safety at Yokohama harbour. The Japanese authorities initially rejected the Vietnamese boat people but later with help from the Red Cross granted them refuge in Kamakura, a hillside retreat for Catholic priests, one hour away from Tokyo.

Nguyen had to leave his home in Vietnam because of feeling threatened by the new communist regime. His father served as an officer in the outgoing government and was thus labelled a friend of the puppet regime. He was to be enlisted for re-education and he and his elder brother would sooner than later be conscripted to fight in the war with Cambodia. So their mother fetched the cash and pleaded of the two boys to flee.

In Japan, a Japanese family adopted Nguyen to be a companion for their only son and the boy was granted official sponsorship. His uncle and aunt who had sailed with him went down the mountain every day to look for work as well as apply for immigration status to one of the four immigrant hosting countries. But the United States and Australia, at the time, refused to accept refugees from Japan, forcing demonstrations by stateless people on the streets. Nguyen's uncle and aunt resorted to prayer. They vowed to

Jeffrey Nguyen (second from left) has a keen interest in the theatre

and somehow some would be traded. Many of them were ill-treated. But in time, the Christian missionaries in Vancouver had set up a home for these distraught girls and rescued Chinese prostitutes and maids.

Nipp also speaks of the Chinese being sent to segregated schools and how segregated schools became part of Chinese memories in Canada for many.

embrace Buddhism. Shortly thereafter came Gerald Regan to change their destinies. Mr. Regan, at the time, was visiting Japan as Canada's Secretary of State. Nguyen's uncle met with him and sought his help. Six months later they were on the plane to Halifax at the invitation of a Baptist Church group.

In Halifax, Nguyen went to school but never fitted in with his class peers because of his age, he recalls. "We were the only Vietnamese family in the area and I remember the cars passing by our benefactor's house in Windsor, would slow down out of curiosity. My uncle wanted us to set a good example so that future Vietnamese in Canada may be judged correctly. I grew conscious of even a sneeze," he says.

The Nguyen's were overwhelmed with the hospitality of their Canadian hosts and felt obliged to be baptized Christians.

Nguyen, who is well-known for his contribution to programs that address the multicultural community's needs, was until last year, the NS Site and National Coordinator of the Cross Cultural Mental Health Initiative facilitating organizational change within the Canada Mental Health Association.

But life as a youth had challenged Nguyen even on Canadian shores. Even until 1983, he was one of only three Asians at Halifax West High School. "'Hey chink,' the boys out there would call me," he remembers. "I wanted to fit in, so I refrained from hanging out with my Asian friends. But that changed nothing. In time, this recognition of the fact that people saw me as a different human being made me severely withdrawn from mainstream life," he says.

Nguyen says that as a consequence he rebelled against his uncle and aunt and ran away from home when he was only sixteen. He rode on a bus to Ottawa. He lived on the streets and slept in the basement of a church. He experienced hunger until it drove him to pawn the Seiko watch the kindly Japanese family had given him.

Life was beginning to be a nightmare, until the RCMP found him and escorted him back to Halifax, lodging him in his home with his uncle and aunt. The "prodigal son" later turned his life around and finished high school.

Nguyen says he rebelled against his uncle and aunt and ran away from home when he was only sixteen. He rode on a bus to Ottawa. He lived on the streets and slept in the basement of a church.

Lumb recalls how a Chinese friend who was shabbily dressed was singled out in class and compared with her. "Often times I felt I should not have been born Chinese because of the way we were treated," she says.

Emma Quon whose mother came to join her merchant husband in Canada in 1913 talks about her friend, Aida, who once confessed being afraid of her. Aida grew up being told by her mother: "If you don't behave, I shall take you to that China man at the laundry."

Under the Willow Tree documents the worst of Chinese memories in Canada. The Chinese Exclusion Act, proclaimed on Dominion Day 1923, halted their immigration, separated families and forced an exodus of about 10,000 Chinese out of Canada. Of course, it was finally repealed in 1947 and the road blocks to family reunification cleared.

The early immigration of Chinese, Japanese and East Indians to Canada's shores at the turn of the century had created a strong anti-Asian antipathy among native Canadian groups and in many ways these developments conspired to push the government toward making immigration policy more restrictive and discriminatory.

As a consequence riots broke out in Vancouver in 1907. The riots, if anything, were a burst of anger smouldering in BC's Asian communities. A giant anti-Asian parade staged on the streets of Vancouver to protest Asian immigration to Canada had ignited the rampage.

Much antipathy was already brewing after reports confirmed that the Grand Trunk Pacific had plans to import thousands of Japanese to work on the railway's western leg. Consequently, the whites began to view the Japanese as threats to their cultural integrity. The

He did his bachelor's degree in health education at Dalhousie University, but realized soon that if health programs were not culturally sensitive in a country where multiculturalism was a stated national policy, then those programs fell short of their goals.

The North End Community Health Centre in Halifax recognized the need for Vietnamese health interpreters and, through government grants, were funded to meet that need. Nguyen was hired.

"I must retain my Vietnamese identity, while being committed to Canada. The seed of the land, may blossom in another, but it will always want to belong to its roots."

Nguyen has been on the Board of Directors of seven organizations focused on immigrant service including Metro United Way, Halifax Peninsula Community Health Board, the Metropolitan Immigrant Settlement Association (MISA) and the Multicultural Association of Nova Scotia (MANS).

In his role as National Coordinator at CMHA, Nguyen was facilitating organizational change through communications, implementing the anti-racism policy in community health boards and ensuring that the recruitment process in the organization was culturally sensitive.

His family, left behind in Vietnam, reunited in Canada twelve years after the separation. But the war in Vietnam that forced him to flee his country did nothing to erode his love for the motherland. "I must retain my Vietnamese identity, while being committed to Canada. The seed of the land, may blossom in another, but it will always want to belong to its roots."

Japanese victory in the Russo-Japanese war of 1905 brought a new dimension to this growing hatred. BC's white residents regarded the Japanese as aggressive, loyal first to Japan and eager to further their country's expansionist goals.

In an attempt to stem the rising immigrant tide, the Trades and Labour Council formed the Asiatic Exclusive League which organized that giant parade to protest. A stone thrown at them from a Chinese store provoked the riots which resulted in extensive damage to buildings.

In the aftermath of the riots, the Laurier government placated the BC government as well as Japan - but in order to appease white British Columbians, it told the Japanese government to limit emigration of its citizens to Canada.

With that out of the way, Mackenzie King, the Minister of Labour, instituted a study of Asian

Cambodian baby flown to Canada in the heat of the war

Sue-San Bopha's narration of the story of her life will remind many of the Old Testament story: The woman, fearing for her son's life, tip-toed to the river with her son Moses in a basket and lowered the child into the water. Then she watched it sail away as she prayed for his safety.

Bopha was born in Cambodia during the heat of the war in 1975 when the invading Khmer Rouge was bombing and devastating the city of Phnom Penh. During the purges of the next four years, one in four Cambodians were sent to the notorious Killing Fields and Bopha could have been one of them.

She was only two weeks old at the time, when in the midst of gunfire and explosions, two caring hands of someone anonymous placed her at the door step of a Phom Penh orphanage called Canada House and left. Along with 43 other children, Bopha was adopted by the orphanage. Canada House is just one of the orphanages under the umbrella of "Families for Children, " a private adoption agency in Ontario with orphanages in several parts of the developing world.

Her flight out of Cambodia a month later was like what one sees in the movies. As buildings crumbled, corpses piled up and shrapnel flew dangerously across the orphanage, Bopha and the other abandoned babies were driven to the airport. They were huddled in a truck that was draped with the Red Cross insignia to escape the vigilant eye of the Khmer Rouge patrols. She flew to Saigon and stayed there for some weeks until a "baby lift" of Indo-Chinese orphans brought her to Canada, to the home of

Sue-San King (centre) with sisters Dolly and Anna Charet

immigration. He attributed the abnormally large numbers to high immigration from Hawaii and to the activities of immigration companies based in Canada.

Consequently, legislation was put in place to ban immigration by way of Hawaii as well as to prohibit companies from importing contract labour. King had also sought to stem the immigrant tide from India.

This was done

Gwen and George King in Edmonton, who raised her with love and affection.

The story would never have been told but for an emotional reunion in Montreal last summer that brought together, almost 26 years later, Sue-San King and the other "grown babies" to meet with sisters Dolly and Anna Charet and Naomi Bronstein who had sheltered the abandoned children in Cambodia during the war.

King moved to Halifax from Edmonton early this year after graduating in modern languages (German and French) at the University of Lethbridge in Alberta. She works as a Research Assistant for the Robertson Surette Group.

King is not bitter about her past. "Although my background hadn't created a sense of curiosity in my teens, I now have the urge to know my roots," says King. "I don't even know if there is one person in my bloodline in Cambodia today. But if I go, it will not be a search for my people....I just want to smell and feel the land I belong to."

She says that if she goes, she may even consider staying back. "I have a deep concern for Cambodian issues, not necessarily Cambodians, and want to work with war-affected children." At once, that observation appears contradictory. But King explains: "The reunion in Montreal was an emotional one, not because I met with Cambodians with a similar fate as mine, but because I met with the people that cared for me. King says she had an emotional one-to-one with sisters Dolly and Anna and with Bronstein. "But as Cambodians, we hardly sat down and shared notes. People think there will be commonalities to share when people of like races meet. But that's not necessarily how it is."

"I have a deep concern for Cambodian issues, not necessarily Cambodians, and want to work with war-affected children." At once, that observation appears contradictory. But King explains: "The reunion in Montreal was an emotional one, not because I met with Cambodians with a similar fate as mine, but because I met with the people that cared for me.

Anyone would think that orphans lack a mother's love. But King refutes that. "I've not felt that lack. I've been given all of it by Gwen and George. It doesn't matter, who gives it to you."

King is also an accomplished singer. A couple of years ago, she travelled extensively to the United States and Europe with the group "Up with People" singing songs about poverty, racism and justice issues. "That was a hands-on experience with global citizenship," she says. "I've had a good time in my life. I'm proud of this progress and this journey."

And somewhere in the world, those caring hands of someone anonymous that placed a baby on the steps of Canada House 26 years ago must be proud too.

by way of an amendment to the Immigration Act. The amendment introduced what came to be known as the "Continuous Journey Regulation" under which potential immigrants would be required to travel to Canada by continuous passage from their country of origin.

Since no shipping company operated a direct service

China-born biochemist manages safe homes for victims of violence

In a corner of the first level of Bloomfield Centre on Agricola Street in Halifax is a room with a view. It's windows open on victims of domestic violence. Its safe homes are for racial minorities, low income immigrants, the physically challenged, gays and lesbians.

At the centre of this work by the Universal Shelter Association, which operates from this room is Chai Chu Thompson, a retired DNA scientist.

Chai-Chu Thompson in a lighter moment

from India to Canadian shores, this ingenious legislation served to ban all Indian immigration.

British Columbia, by virtue of facing the Pacific Ocean, drew many of its non-British newcomers from Asia, including Japan at the turn of the nineteenth century. By 1914, however, only 10,000 Japanese had settled in the whole of Canada, by far the largest number in British Columbia.

The first wave of Japanese immigrants, called Issei, arrived between 1877 and 1928. Prior to 1907, most Japanese settlers were young men. In that year, at Canada's insistence, Japan limited the number of males who could emigrate to this country to 400 a year, thereby becoming the only nation to specifically control the movement of its people to Canada.

The Issei were invariably young and came from poor and overcrowded fishing and farming villages.

Thompson's work against injustice was acclaimed by Flare Magazine's Lifetime Achievement Award a few years ago. The volunteer awards honour Canadian women who have dedicated time to enrich the lives of others. Thompson's life, as she says, has been balanced between career as a scientist and work as a humanist.

Born in Southern China, Thompson's family moved to Taiwan during the revolution. But a biochemist by training, Thompson later studied at Yale, where she met her husband Tony, whose job at Dal University brought the couple to Halifax in 1966.

Thompson co-founded the Universal Shelter Association with seven other people who broke away from the board of another shelter after evidence of racial discrimination in the workplace. Thus while Universal Shelter provides safe homes to all, it especially serves racial minorities and the disadvantaged groups in our society.

It's a volunteer organization that operates with a budget of about $35,000 raised mostly by fund-raising campaigns. Thompson says the organization has some 14 volunteer safe homes, one of which is her own. These are transition homes that provide a maximum stay of a week.

"It's about the time it takes for victims of abuse to recover emotionally and find alternative housing," says Thompson. "During that transition, we do what we can, providing counsel, referral, emotional support, accompanying our clients to the courts or applying for their social assistance," she says.

An immigrant herself, she knows what it is to be in those shoes. The barriers that immigrants come up against with language and culture shock make them disadvantaged in our society. "In some of these cases, all that is compounded by violence at home," she says.

The early immigrants, veterans of the Canadian Army from the First World War and the Canadian-born children suffered the harsh bruises of a racist society and were subject to massive discriminatory legislation, which meant being excluded from employment in specific industrial sectors and trades.

During World War 1, opponents of Asian immigration in BC argued that Japanese children were a threat to the health and progress of white children and should be removed from schools. But despite the pressure, the school board stood its ground.

Nonetheless, matters got worse when Japan bombed Pearl Harbour on December 7, 1941. Canada invoked the War Measures Act and stripped Japanese-Canadians of their civil rights. The government ordered their removal from the West Coast and in the following year about 20,000 Japanese Canadians were despatched to internment camps.

Thompson says her shelter particularly caters to minorities because they are the ones left out. "The homes in Halifax either serve women facing violence at home or homeless youth under the age of 19," she says. "A gay youth over the age of 19, for example, who becomes a victim of parental violence, would thus have no where to go."

Since start-up, the shelter has served so many people of different backgrounds in need of a transition home.

Thompson has received other awards for her volunteer work. In 1995, the Department of Citizenship and Immigration honoured her with a Citation for Citizenship – an award that honours the contribution of people in work that served to integrate newcomers into mainstream Canadian life.

Away from the shelter, Thompson takes up issues of injustice – inequities faced by immigrant women in education and employment.

But although Thompson volunteers for about 16,000 hours a year at Universal Shelter, she still makes time to care for her four grandchildren. She is mother to three children – a daughter who practices medicine in Boston, and two sons, a computer scientist and a mechanical engineer.

Away from the shelter, Thompson takes up issues of injustice – inequities faced by immigrant women in education and employment.

Novelist Joy Kogowa, born to Japanese Canadian parents in 1935, poignantly tells the story in her novel Obasan, which is a portrayal of the Japanese-Canadian evacuation, internment and dispersal during World War II when Canada was at war with Japan.

When in 1942 the whole coast of BC was cleared of anyone of Japanese descent, Kogowa was put on a train and shipped to Slocan where she lived in a dingy hut. Today, in Toronto, she works to restore the damaged pride of a people immensely loyal to a country that betrayed them.

David Suzuki (1936) who through his radio and TV programs introduced scientific concepts to the people of Canada, suffered the same humility as did author Shizuye Takashima (1928) who like Suzuki, although born of Canadian-born parents, was interned in camps.

Japanese-Canadian author turns to activism

Joy Kogawa is not today's immigrant. She is a second-generation Japanese Canadian. But her early experience of life in Canada, the evacuation to Slocan in BC during World War II and the internment are quite akin to the sting of bigotry that some of today's immigrants identify with.

Kogawa pursued studies in education at the University of Alberta and taught elementary school in Coaldale for a year. She then studied music at the University of Toronto and at the Anglican Women's Training College and later at the University of Saskatchewan

Kogawa has won fame as a novelist. But today she is an activist increasingly involved in taking up social justice issues. Her book *Obasan,* which won several book awards, focuses on Japanese Canadians and the injustices they were subjected to during and after the Second World War, when Japan bombed Pearl Harbour. The protagonist in the book is Naomi and in her second novel *Itsuka*, the story continues and concentrates on the emotional and political involvement of Naomi in the Japanese-Canadian redress movement.

Kogawa was involved, some years ago, in seeking redress from the Canadian government for the internment of 20,000 Japanese Canadians during World War II. She was subsequently made a Member of the Order of Canada.

How does Kogawa feel about roots and nationhood. "The deepest roots are the ones involving one's deepest beliefs," she says. "Speaking of my identity, I would probably not consider my deepest identity to be my nationality."

As a child, she says she did, however, develop a sense of Canadian identity because her

The 1996 census recorded a total of 77,130 Japanese Canadians.

The Japanese influence is greatest, however, on the West coast in the fisheries and agriculture sectors. But second and third generation Japanese are typically more professionally trained and bring to the workforce a cadre of highly skilled engineers and administrators.

The Japanese have integrated successfully with mainstream Canadian life, but as a community they rally together toward common causes.

In the 1980s the community focused much of its energy lobbying for the redress of wartime wrongs which the federal government acknowledged and made good through compensations to those deprived of rights and freedoms in Canada during World War II. Japanese Canadians today are somewhat

parents chose not to create alienation and wanted Canadian identity for the siblings.

"Though we were sent to those camps and segregated, we were still very patriotic to Canada. We loved McKenzie King, the Prime

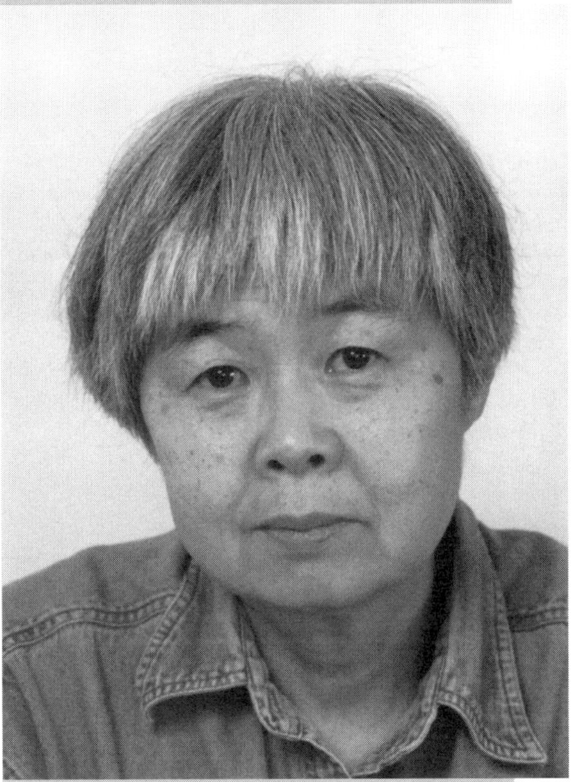

Joy Kogawa Photo: John Flanders

Minister who said once that it was fortunate the bombs fell on Japan and not on Europe. We sang the Maple leaf forever."

Ultimately, Kogawa says, what endures in the psyche is the basic human values of compassion.

She questions the road Canada is taking today. "The country is changing. That is why *represented in Canada's political life.*

Many have distinguished careers as scientists such as geneticist and broadcaster David Suzuki.

As a leading scientist in Canada, Suzuki began a series of TV programs in BC. The program "Suzuki On Science" became a popular serial - produced by CBC TV.

His own work was in the field of genetics – the science dealing with how living things grow and develop – and was helping scientists learn how to reproduce exact copies of a particular organism.

Japanese architect Raymond Moriyama has international fame as do writers and poets Roy Miki, Joy Kogawa and Rick Shiomi.

Canadian missionaries had begun pastoral work in the historic Hamgyong province of Korea in 1898. But there was little Korean immigration to Canada prior to Word War II. If anything, the Korean war

wherever we see groups struggling for social justice, I see hope."

She sees the widening gap between the rich and the poor and is currently working on a community currency – an evolving form of money that communities can create for themselves. "If we are on the Titanic, we might hit the iceberg anytime," she says. "Those involved in community currencies are doing more than creating deck chairs, instead they're building Noah's rafts."

Kogawa quotes Bertrand Russell, who said that friendship was his most significant accomplishment. She believes in the value of relationship and connectedness. "The main word for my journey is TRUST," she says. "It's the thing that matters the most. In the foreground of my mind, I keep a basic trust that love exists towards us and despite the evidence of evil, I trust love will win."

"The main word for my journey is TRUST," she says. "It's the thing that matters the most. In the foreground of my mind, I keep a basic trust that love exists towards us and despite the evidence of evil, I trust love will win."

Kogawa says that recently she has been thinking that the nature of reality is porous. Insights, light, understanding come to us through the porousness, through the openness and through our connection especially to the suffering in the world.

Her most recent novel, The Rain Ascends, deals with an emotional issue of a different kind: the sexual abuse of children by a Protestant clergyman.

which sent northerners fleeing toward the south as refugees, may have resulted in some emigration. By about 1967 formal diplomatic relations had also been established with Korea. The 1996 census of Canada recorded a total of 66,655 people claiming Korean ancestry – the majority of Koreans, however, reside in Ontario.

Koreans are represented in all sectors of the workforce as physicians, accountants and college and university teachers although many are also entrepreneurs managing restaurants, travel agencies and real estate offices.

In Toronto one can see a Korean small business neighbourhood on Bloor Street West where Korean restaurants, bakeries, gift shops and travel agencies have mushroomed. In tandem, Korean conglomerates have set up branch offices in Canada, the most notable

Korean businessman brings Korean investments into Canada

In Chang Kang's office, you see a greeting card which commemorates July 21, 1998 as the centenary of the First Canadian missionaries that went to Korea and established the country's first Christian church. That centenary was celebrated in Halifax three years ago on December 6, with greetings brought by United Christian leaders and the Lt. Governor of Nova Scotia. As part of the celebrations, a plaque was installed at the Saint Columbus Chapter of the Atlantic School of Philosophy.

Kang came to Halifax only thirteen years ago on an exploratory visit sponsored by the Canadian embassy. He saw that the small businesses some new immigrants had ventured into was not to his liking. Kang was managing Hyundai's regional operations in Africa at the time and his children were studying in London.

Unimpressed with the opportunities in Ontario, he filed emigration papers at the UK embassy. But Kang says: "Canada was not happy to see me go." An immigration officer with Citizenship and Immigration Canada in Toronto presented him with several options in

He began a trading operation in Halifax but later responded to the government's suggestion that he should play a role in wooing investments from Hong Kong and Korea. "If we have 1,000 people like you we should have no problem developing this region," the official told Kang.

being Hyundai and Samsung, while three Korean banks – Korea Exchange, Chohung and Hanil credit unions have set up operations as well.

The Korea Times Daily, New Korea Times and Korea News are the three most prominent Korean newspapers in Canada, but there are also Korean language broadcasting stations that can be found in the larger settlement areas. The churches (United and Presbyterian) are central to Korean community life. But, of course, there are also a substantial number of Roman Catholics and Buddhists – devoted adherents of Korea's dominant religion.

The Korean associations in Toronto, Winnipeg, Edmonton, and Vancouver administer several cultural fairs – notable among them are the Caravan in Toronto, Folklorama in Winnipeg, the Heritage Festival in Edmonton, and the Asian Music Festival in Vancouver.

Chang Kang

Canada's other provinces. "Nova Scotia topped our list. A director at the Nova Scotia Department of Economic Development and Tourism invited me to a meeting and showed me the opportunities. My immigration papers were processed rapidly," Kang says.

He began a trading operation in Halifax initially but later responded to the government's recommendation that his company should play a role in wooing investments from Hong Kong and Korea. "If we have 1,000 people like you we should have no problem developing this region," the government official told Kang.

Kang's company was a runaway success as an investment catalyst. Substantial investments came in from Hong Kong and were spread across Canada, including some

When in 1975, the communist North overran South Vietnam, at least 150,000 Vietnamese fled the country and resettled in the United States, France, and Canada.

Canada was humanitarian in its response to the plight of the Vietnamese, Laotians, and Kampucheans who fled Communist regimes in the wake of Saigon's fall in 1975.

The Khymer Rouge- the Communist Party of Cambodia, had unleashed a reign of terror between 1975 and 1978 led by Pol Pot.

Vietnam ended that reign when it invaded Cambodia, but in turn provoked a war with China. As hostilities mounted, some 700,000 ethnic Chinese from the North fled the country between 1978 and 1982.

In 1979 and 1980, Canada accepted approximately 60,000 of these refugees, most of whom had endured several days in small,

investments in the Bayer's Lake industrial area of Metro Halifax. Kang twice accompanied Nova Scotia's premier to Korea and once participated in Team Canada's foray into Korea. "I brought in money, people and businesses into Canada - creating several joint ventures including a salmon hatchery in the Annapolis Valley, another trading group- the Old Orchard Inn in Wolfville, Big Four Fisheries, Charter Real Estate Advisors and so on," he says.

The pace at which Korean investments poured in may have influenced the Nova Scotia government's decision to proclaim Korea Day on October 8, 1994.

Young Korean saw a future in the English-speaking world

I.K. Hwang is bringing Canadians and Koreans together and in the process not only creating cross-cultural understanding but creating economic spinoffs for both.

Hwang does not let life shape things for him. He shapes life for himself. Graduating from university in Korea where he studied electronics engineering, Hwang was looking at factors that would change the shape of things to come over the next ten years and realized that while computers and technology were going to lead that way, the processing of all information would happen mostly in English.

"Today jet engines power our planes, but tomorrow atomic engines could probably take planes across the world in a tenth of that time, I figured," he says. "But I realized that if I must be at the cutting edge, I should work in a native *leaky boats, prey to vicious pirate attacks, before ending up in squalid camps in Thailand and Malaysia.*

Their numbers were such that they comprised 25 percent of all the newcomers to this country between 1978 and 1981.

The movement of the boat people to Canada, in fact, gained momentum in 1978. Its springboard was the announcement that Canada would offer a home to 600 refugees on board the Hai Hong, which the Malaysian government had refused permission to dock.

In the following year, there was a dramatic increase in the number of refugees fleeing Vietnam. In response to intensive lobbying by church congregations, the government led by Conservative leader Joe Clark, announced that it would admit 50,000 refugees to Canada by the end of 1980.

Thanks to the Clark government's generous response, some 77,000 Indo-

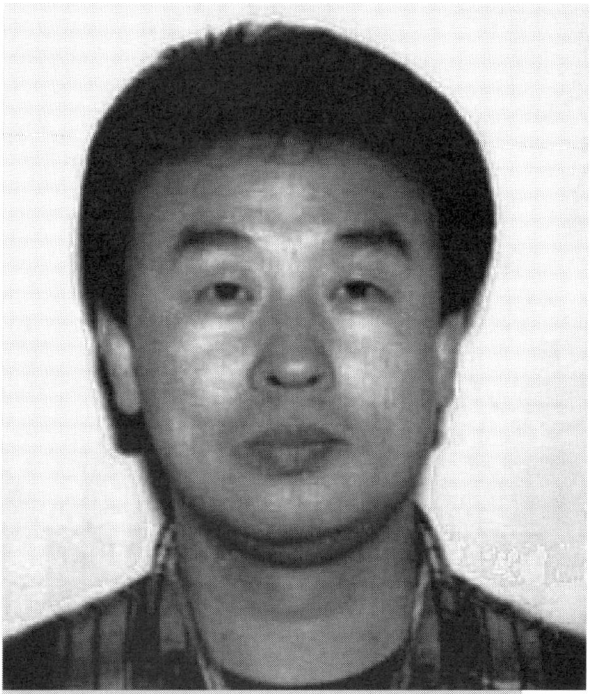

I.K.Hwang: catalyst bringing Korean ESL schools and Canadian language institutes together

English environment."

He quit his job in the Testing Department of the Consumer Protection Board, where he says he was bored with routine and the lack of challenge and took courses in English while kindling the urge to emigrate out of Korea.

Hwang obviously had some choices, but he chose Canada because "it has more humanity than the United States of America." But while choosing Canada, he opted not for British Columbia or even Ontario, the provinces with a greater concentration of Koreans. "I wanted an environment where I knew nobody, just for the challenge."

Koreans invest great sums of money in their children's English language education, says

Chinese refugees entered Canada between 1975 and 1981.

Vietnamese Canadians have spread out across Canada. The new arrivals have set up enterprises including restaurants and food processing companies while many are herbalists and acupuncture specialists.

The Vietnamese in Canada have created strong group support systems in order to propitiate a national culture in exile through a combination of student societies, professional, religious and political organizations.

Têt, the lunar New Year is celebrated in late January, to commemorate the war dead. In many ways religion also groups the community together.

Buddhism and Christianity are the two major religions of the Vietnamese. The Buddhist temples are central to their community life.

Hwang. So while he put aside electronics engineering for the time being, he set up a business that made arrangements for the export of Canadian teachers to Korea. He established links with English-as-a-Second Language (ESL) institutes in Korea and started to recruit Canadian English teachers.

The program got off the ground quite successfully and Hwang, last winter, introduced a camping program. He travelled across Nova Scotia to identify camping environments and collaborated with organizations from Dalhousie, Saint Mary's and Mount Saint Vincent's universities and the YMCA in Halifax. In partnerships with Korean organizations, last year, Hwang hosted a group of 51 Korean children who came to Canada with four chaperons. These camps brought in a substantial amount of money into Canada, he says.

But he remains happy and unhappy at the same time. "Happy, because I have achieved something. Unhappy, because the people I love most choose not to come to Canada," he says.

Early this year, Hwang was collaborating with an English language institute to provide support services to their ESL and Host programs and has been catalytic in bringing Korean ESL schools and Canadian language institutes together. Hwang plays a role as well, teaching the Korean language to Canadian English teachers who are training before travel to Korea.

In the five years that Hwang has been in Canada, he has networked extensively and has never had the time to feel lonely, he says. But he remains happy and unhappy at the same time. "Happy, because I have achieved something. Unhappy, because the people I love most choose not to come to Canada," he says.

Filipino helps fellow countrymen touch base with home

Oppression, marshal law, economic instability and low employment during Ferdinand Marcos' regime in the Philippines brought Armando Regala to Canada in 1977.

Regala did not quite miss the bus - the first Filipino immigrants came to Nova Scotia only in the early Sixties - among them two prominent medical professionals who made a significant contribution as pathologist at the Victoria General Hospital and as forensic psychiatrist at the Halifax Infirmary. In later years, as Regala remembers, many Filipinos came to Nova Scotia as live-in caregivers from Hong Kong and Singapore and later applied for landed immigrant status.

Today with more than five hundred Filipino families in Nova Scotia, the community contributes significantly through its medical technicians, nurses, architects and engineers, educators and other trades people.

Like many immigrants, Regala sought a junior position as administrative secretary to the Dean of Architecture at Dalhousie University, where today he still serves as the Benefits Administrator for some 3,000 employees. Looking back, he recognizes the fact that career growth was not as rapid as he would have desired it to be. "One does not know why that is true. The bosses do not discriminate, they treat you like an equal. But culturally diverse people, although very qualified, somehow do not seem to rise above a certain management threshold," he observes.

Nonetheless, Regala is a happy man and a busy one. As President of the Multicultural Council of Halifax/Dartmouth (MCHD), he jumpstarted two very important programs, one focused on leadership training for

Armando Regala: If I live without making a difference, I have lived in vain

immigrant youth and the other on academic credentials and needs assessment, while also calling for a conference on racism.

But as he came to learn later, racism is not all black and white. The ethnic groups within the MCHD held fast to their own agendas. His mandate as President was to enhance the working structure of the organization so as to make it catalytic in the immigrant community's effort to integrate within main stream Canadian society.

His frustration over not being able to effect change there saw the birth of the Centre for Diverse Visible Cultures (CDVC). He chairs this government-funded organization whose mandate is to help people from diverse cultures integrate and become contributors to Canadian society.

Filipinos have strong family ties and feel strongly committed to financially assist their families in the Philippines, whether by paying medical bills or university tuition fees, he explains.

That explains why the major revenues in the Philippines come from remittances. Regala may have gone home only twice in twenty seven years, but he is developing a family tree through a software programme so as to give his three children a sense of their "roots".

In quite the same way, he also helps fellow Filipinos touch base with home through a website that he and two other friends in the United States have created. It's a home page for all Filipinos who trace their origin to Kapampangam, the most prominent of the country's regions when the Spaniards came to the Philippines.

"Today we take great pride in Kapampangam culture and recognize the need to preserve its heritage," he says. The web page has sections dedicated to the language, poetry, folk song, cuisine, mythology, flora and fauna of the region. It also has dedicated pages for the National Council of Canadian Filipino Associations, Knights of Risal and the CDVC.

Regala believes we all have a role to play. "If I live without making a difference, I will have lived in vain. I must leave the world a better place than I found it," he says.

Regala believes we all have a role to play. "If I live without making a difference, I will have lived in vain. I must leave the world a better place than I found it," he says.

MP narrows gaps in China-Canada relations

Sophia Leung, Canada's first Asian woman in parliament, says she is not famous, only hardworking.

Sophia has written *Discover China* and a *Treasury of Chinese Art* as well as edited the book *S. Wah Leung: A Celebration of Life* which is a testament to her late husband and contains stories by Dr. S. Wah Leung's students, colleagues and friends. In her books as well as in her other work, Leung has tried to be a catalyst in developing an understanding between Canada and China.

Sophia Leung, MP

About roots and nationhood, Leung says: "Canada is my country, no two ways. But there are sentiments attached to China and Taiwan where I was born and raised. There is no identity conflict. I have been fortunate to combine the values of both cultures and distill it into what I am."

Leung says Pierre Trudeau was a great man with a vision. "He had said once: 'We must have a just society, true racial equality. We have to respect the rights of others.' That set the tone in Canada for the emergence of a multicultural society. I believe Canada has been built by the strength of immigrants and that we must therefore be treated equally. We must give our children a just society."

Before Leung plunged into politics, she was always a people's person, she says, trying to effect change in the community and facilitating integration so as to give meaning to multiculturalism and bring about true acceptance of our differences. "I was trained as a social worker. So I am involved not only with the Chinese community but with communities at large."

Leung says she does not feel bitter about the past when the

Chinese were badly treated. "I think we must learn from history. I do not want to condone bigots. But there is no urge to punish the dead. You know about the *Komatgata Maru* incident. We must seek to correct – so that we may never see that happen again."

Speaking about success, Leung says she is still very humble. "I travelled to the US at the age of 18 with very little money. I was taking great risks. But I had a goal. At all times I ask myself: Why am I here? What am I doing? Where am I headed? I do not count my accomplishments. I do not believe life is about living it up and driving big cars. I did think of going back to China at some time in order to serve my community there. But I am not a communist, so I chose not to.

Leung is happy in the political arena because it gives her an opportunity to effect change. "There is so much more to be done – look at the obstacles in the way for women, then imagine how much worse it is for women who are visible minorities," she says.

She has been awarded the Order of Canada. Leung has traveled with Prime Minister Jean Chretien to China to bridge gaps and now she's playing another role, that of creating twin cities between China and Canada.

A Parliamentary Secretary to the Minister of National Revenue Sophia was born in Wuxi, China. In 1948, she and her family moved to Taiwan. From there she travelled to the United States to earn her Bachelor of Science Degree from the University of Pittsburgh, Pa. In 1962, she and her husband - the late Dr. S. Wah Leung, O.C. - moved to Vancouver, B.C. where Dr. Leung established the Faculty of Dentistry at the University of BC.

Leung received her Master's Degree in Social Work at UBC. She worked as a medical social worker for 15 years in Vancouver area hospitals and was involved in research and teaching. As a community activist, Leung has served on the Board of Directors with over 20 arts, business, and community organizations. In recognition of her contributions, she has received numerous government awards.

During her first year as Member of Parliament she served as Chair of the B.C. Liberal Caucus and Vice-Chair of the Northern and Western Caucus. In addition, she is the Vice-Chair of the Canada-China Legislative Friendship Association, and member of the Canada - Europe Friendship Association, Canada - Cuba Friendship Association, Canadian NATO Parliamentary Association, and also the Canada-Ireland Friendship Group. In July of 1999, Ms. Leung was part of the Canadian government delegation to the OSCE Parliamentary Assembly in St. Petersburg, Russia.

In September 1999 she travelled to China with the Chair of the Foreign Affairs Committee. In April 2000, the MP went on a mission with the Hon. Elinor Caplan, the Minister of Citizenship & Immigration to China. For the fall 2000 session of parliament, the Prime Minister appointed Sophia Leung Parliamentary Secretary to the Minister of National Revenue. Ms. Leung was re-elected to represent the Vancouver-Kingsway riding on November 27, 2000

In February 2001, she travelled with Prime Minister Chretien and TEAM Canada to China. Later in April, she represented Canada to officially open the Group of Seven Canadian Art Exhibition in Beijing, Canada.

feel Chinese even though I have no intention of returning.

Discoverer of T-cell Receptor has mixed feelings about nationhood.

Mak Tak: discoverer of T-Cell receptors

Until the Sixties, Hong Kong was still very strongly a colony of Great Britain where Chinese were seen as second citizens, says Mak Tak, the man who discovered the T-Cell Receptor. "The US was thus seen as the land of opportunity for many Chinese in Hong Kong."

Nonetheless, Tak says, the political situation and the cold war and Vietnam left one wondering about the price of a US imposed democracy. Canada was a kinder and gentler nation.

Tak says he has mixed feelings about nationhood." I still do

"Canada is my chosen land where I have worked, matured as an individual, in a country of opportunities and social responsibility. I am very proud and comfortable here and this is also a country where my family was raised. I do not feel ultra nationalistic but I am proud to be a Canadian," he says.

Tak says discovering T cell receptors was without doubt the major milestone in his career. "Our recent work on Hodgkins also gives me hope for developing a new treatment for this cancer."

T-cell receptors are molecules on our immune cells that can differentiate between foreign (pathogens) and self antigens, Tak explains. "This distinction allows our body to attack viruses, bacteria and parasites and leave our own tissues from self attack, thus preventing infections and autoimmune diseases."

Success, Tak says, is a relative thing. " I would not say we are successful in science. We all try to make progress and will not know for many years the implications of each discovery. "

Having been around and making progress gives me the confidence that I can continue to provide a breeding ground for young talented investigators to learn and practice science.

Hong Kong-born Senator says diversity enriches Canada

Senator Vivienne Poy

Vivienne Poy, a Senator in Canada, says she has never felt she had national roots. "I was Chinese in a British colony (Hong Kong) where I had no vote. Thus, although, I may be Chinese culturally, I am not truly Chinese because I do not identify with Chinese politics."

But Poy says her emotions changed when she became Canadian. "I felt that, at last, I had a country to call my own," she says. She came to Canada as a student, met her husband and stayed. Prior to coming here, she had lived in residence at a school in England and therefore never did experience the typical settlement problems, especially connected with language barriers and exposure to an individualistic society.

Poy says she never wanted to be in politics, nor has she ever joined a political party. "Thus, when my nomination to the Senate was announced, I was the first to be surprised," she says.

Prior to becoming a Senator, Poy was a fashion designer who marketed her merchandise both in Canada and overseas to countries such as Puerto Rico, Hawaii, Japan and the United States. Even today, she manages a couple of private companies.

At a time when everything is being globalized - the economy, travel, everything - why not globalize people?

Poy believes Canada is unique in the way it welcomes people from diverse cultures, and encourages them to keep their cultures alive. "I do believe we enrich Canada with what we bring to this country. But there will always be segments of the population who oppose immigration. At a time when everything is being globalized - the economy, travel, everything - why not globalize people?" she asks.

What does Poy count among her achievements? "I do not count my achievements," she says. "It's not for me to look back at them, it's for others to do that. If I volunteer for projects, it's not to gain brownie points, but because I truly love people and like to help."

Some time ago, Poy ventured out to look for her roots and the exercise resulted in a book: *A River Named Lee*. "The book is about my ancestors," she says. "I wanted to know where my Chinese name came from. I have a keen sense of history, and decided to ask the older generation about my roots. I was fortunate to find that there were ancestral records, and was able to trace my family history back 2000 years. I interviewed people, and did historical research on the record of early dynasties, and the migration of my ancestors."

Later, Poy wrote a second book about her father's life. Poy's father grew up in Hong Kong. When the British colony was being transformed after World War II, he was a member of the legislative and executive councils.

The most important thing he did was to build bridges for Hong Kong and China with Europe and Japan. "He was among the first to bring investments into China. When Hong Kong did not have water, he spoke to the Chinese government, and they agreed to pipe the water from the East River to Hong Kong, although credit for this decision was ultimately given to Hong Kong's governor," Poy observes.

Senator Poy has three children - Ashley, a social worker with a teacher's degree, Justin, an artist and entrepreneur, and Carter, who got his business degree in Canada, and works in China.

Emigration out of South Asia

Emigration out of South Asia

The first South Asians, mostly Sikhs from the Punjab, settled in British Columbia at the turn of the century. In 1907, at least 5,000 Punjabis are reported to have found work in British Columbia and opposition to their presence by Canadians once again prompted the government to introduce discriminatory legislation.

In BC, in the late nineteenth century, the school boards held the view that Asians neither could nor should be assimilated. At about that time, several provinces passed statutes restricting the settlement of Asians. The law even forbade Asians from voting.

The most hated anti-Asian legislation introduced at the time was the one that made sailing on a "continuous journey" from a port in

Indian entrepreneur says roots are not a geographical notion

Masoom Hamza's diary makes some definite distinctions about cultural idiosyncrasies. Overwhelmed by a brand new culture upon coming to Canada, she says: "We need the rules, the system, the respect. The love for truth. I am happy. I am busy. I am learning. I am free. I am me, like God intended. Finally."

A firebrand from India, steeped in the ways of that world, always on top of it, Hamza had realized one afternoon at a pub in

Masoom Hamza

India mandatory for immigration.

As is well-known, the 376 passengers aboard the ship called the Komagata Maru which challenged the regulation and entered Vancouver were denied the right to disembark and finally deported.

Canadian immigration law has come a long way, since, with landmark legislation reflected in the Immigration Act of 1976 which tore down the erstwhile race-based piece of legislation. Consequently, about a million immigrants came to Canada in the first half of the nineties according to the 1996 census. The switch in emphasis to occupation and skills, instead of race, has brought more people from Asia rather than Europe as was the case 30 years ago.

Today's new immigrants come from Hong Kong China, India, Pakistan, The Philippines, Iran and Sri Lanka, while traditional sources of immigrants such as Europe are giving way to Latin

Vancouver that her country wasn't cutting it because its ethos, per se, was corrupting. Canada was like a breath of fresh air.

Hamza, who was managing her own Art Store in Dubai before she came to Canada some months ago says she isn't ashamed to leave India and adopt Canada as her own. "I have to find the pride in being a good human being first," she says.

She thinks roots are not a geographical notion. "It's what I have inherited. So it can travel with me. I realize that with my roots, I bring to Canada a set of values. But then, I want to drop the rest of the baggage – the pettiness, the crookedness, the shortcuts, the deception. Now that I am in Canada, rather than crib about everything, I want to, instead, absorb. I may have to start at the very beginning – like learning to walk down the aisle in a supermarket without dropping something."

She thinks Canadians have a sense of pride, though they don't make it obvious. "They prove it in the strength of character. They live by values and heart. No hype. Truth is what you get. They are not naive but open. They are smart but kind. They believe and so invite belief."

Hamza explains the disparities quite well. She says that in her own country she's got to work with survival tools – all of which make you corrupt and deceptive. She thinks there are no survival problems in Canada – well at least not of the magnitude one finds in the developing world, so you get to live what you are.

She'll be setting up business soon. She says she came here with misconceptions and ignorance. But having researched, she now has the facts. "I'm ready to join the game." In Vancouver, small business is big business and Hamza is happy that our governments realize entrepreneurs have wider aspirations. "I've seen so many from the Middle East come to Canada and do very well.

America and Africa. Today at least 750,000 people living in Canada can trace their cultural roots to South Asia, including present-day India, Pakistan, Bangladesh, and Sri Lanka.

Emigrants from India represent a highly skilled work-force of IT professionals, doctors and engineers as well as academics who have energized Canada's universities, the civil service, hospitals, and high-tech industries. Despite some setbacks, Indian Canadians as a group have an average income approximately equal to the Canadian average.

Many political candidates of Indian heritage have successfully run at the provincial and federal levels. British Columbia politicians, the Hon. Herb Dhaliwal, M.P., Minister of Fisheries and Oceans, and Reform Party member, the Hon. Gurmant Grewal have served at the federal level. Reform M.Ps Deepak Obhrai and Rahim Jaffer represent

Hamza does not deny the fact that a crop of Indians are known for their brilliance in information technology or science or medicine. But her observation on that is philosophical: "That may be so. But why are we brilliant Indians coming to Canada," she asks. "The brilliance must filter down to basic life. Canadians have the smart systems in place to make sure they have a home and a bed from which they can wake up smiling, have a job to go to, a car to drive around, a government that's accountable. At the end of the day, smart people must create smart environments, must work towards building trust and honesty, achieving peace," she says. "At Canadian libraries, you swipe your own videos and leave. Now, where in the world would you find such trust."

The west has been criticized for its promiscuous society by conservative communities in South East Asia. But Hamza says she would raise her children here. "Of course I will. We are trained to choose our options. On the other hand what do you mean by promiscuity? We too have fallen and stumbled as we grew up."

The West has been criticized for its promiscuous society by conservative communities in South East Asia. But Hamza says she would raise her children here. "Of course I will. We are trained to choose our options. On the other hand what do you mean by promiscuity? We too have fallen and stumbled as we grew up."

ridings in Alberta.

In Ontario Gurbax Malhi has served the federal riding of Malton as a Liberal Party M.P. British Columbia has four MLAs of Indian heritage including Sindi Hawkins, Moe Sihota, Harry Lali, and Ujjal Dosanjh who, as leader of British Columbia's NDP, became Premier of British Columbia in February 2000- the first Indo-Canadian to hold that office in Canada - and served until May 2001.

Hinduism, Sikhism, Islam, Buddhism, Christianity, Jainism, Judaism, and Zoroastrianism - all have adherents within Canada's Indian population. In Ontario, some 50 temples serve the needs of Hindus. Sikh gurdwaras, notably in British Columbia and Ontario, are central to their community development.

Among the expanding Muslim communities in Canada are the Ismailis who have built a network of social institutions and who are linked to the Aga Khan and his institutions. The first mosque in Canada

First Indian to be elected Premier in Canada

When Ujjal Dosanjh was a young boy, his grandfather would take him out on a wooden cart in his hometown in the northern Indian state of the Punjab and tell him stories about *Kamagata Maru*, the gurdwara reform movement and heroes of India's freedom movement, Mahatma Gandhi and Jawaharlal Nehru. He says, at some point, those stories impacted solidly and steered his thinking towards higher and nobler goals.

Ujjal Dosanjh

Kamagata Maru, as must be recalled, was the Japanese steamer that an influential Sikh, Gurdit Singh, had leased in order to bring some 376 East Indians, mostly Punjabis, to Vancouver and challenge the "continuous journey" regulation that the Canadian government had introduced to bar East Indian immigration.

Dosanjh, who came to Canada from the Punjab as a young man of 20, was elected Premier of Britsh Columbia in February 2000.

Dosanjh told crowds at the time, that the

was erected in Edmonton in 1938. But by the 1980s mosques were found all across Canada

Sri Lankan immigration to Canada began after the Second World War and more significantly after Canada revised its immigration policy in 1967 making skills and not race the criteria. In the 1996 Canadian census, 31,435 persons indicated that they were of Sri Lankan heritage. It is likely that this figure is made up primarily of the island's two dominant groups, the Sinhalese and Burghers. As well, 30,065 individuals declared themselves in census reports to be of Tamil origin –a third group that is fighting for independence.

The exodus of the Burghers out of Sri Lanka began when English as the official language was dethroned and the Burghers felt marginalized as a result.

The Sinhalese, mostly English educated, too, came in search of employment and social opportunities.

election of a once ordinary immigrant worker to such a high position showed the commitment of the Canadian people.

Dosanjh left India when he was 17 and travelled to England to study. "But I didn't have the money and so I took up part-time jobs to pay for my schooling," he says. Three years later in 1968, while strolling alongside the Canadian High Commission in London, he decided on impulse to apply for immigrant status. He ended up in Vancouver.

"Don't let anyone tell you that as an immigrant he didn't feel a sense of turmoil in the moving process," Dosanjh says. "It's no easy thing to leave a country. I felt a sense of void. But, of course, in time I began to live a full life."

He initially went to work at a lumber mill in Vancouver while he studied at a night school. A few months later an injury at the mill put him out of school and work for about a year. But he bounced back and finally finished his Bachelor of Arts degree and graduated in Law from the University of BC.

Dosanjh says: "I didn't wake up one morning and tell myself "let's get into politics." Activism, he says, has been a life-long interest. "I've always spoken out for farm worker's rights, racism and human rights issues" he says. In Britain, Dosanjh had formed an organization of young Indians to advocate for causes. In Vancouver he joined the NDP while he worked for a lumber mill.

Not happy to speak about his work in BC while he served first as Attorney General and later as Premier, Dosanjh says he has modestly helped to effect change. One can see that, he says, in the protection that farm workers in British Columbia get from the Employment Standards legislation. "I have helped to improve the Human Rights Act

But since the decade of the 80s, the Tamil insurgency and the campaign for independence in Sri Lanka had created bloody civil strife and forced an exodus of both genuine and economic refugees.

Canada responded to the crisis by creating a special Tamil refugee settlement program in 1989 and admitted them in.

Nearly all Sinhalese, Burgher and Tamil immigrants in Canada have settled in urban areas, especially Ontario, although smaller concentrations of Sri Lankans are contributing to the growth of urban communities in Quebec, Alberta, and British Columbia.

The early immigrants have continued in professional, technical, or managerial positions in Canada, whereas most of the post-1983 arrivals set up small businesses. Among Sri Lankan Canadians, the poet and writer Michael Ondaatje is probably the most well known. He has helped put Canadian literature on the

in BC and introduce hate legislation, deal with equality for gays and lesbians, legislate for pay equity for women and lower the tuition fees at BC universities.

Of course, as is known to many, Dosanjh moved out of the Premier's office when he lost the elections in May 2001. "I'm going to do some cleaning up around in the house, shake the dust off my books and reconnect with family for the next few months," he says.

Dosanjh says there is no question about where his loyalties are. "Canada is my home and my loyalties are to Canada. But India is close to my heart." The former premier says he feels strongly about his heritage, the country he ran away from. "All that gives me a sense of inculpability about myself."

What has success taught him? "Life is not only about success and accomplishment," he observes. "It's being able to go on this journey of life feeling satisfied for doing what one has wanted to," he says.

Indian psychologist loses his Sikh identity in Canada

Dr. Sid Sodhi's leftist political ideas, which got rooted in his college years in India's northern state of the Punjab, saw him in and out of trouble with government bureaucrats. By then the young man was flaunting a Bachelor's degree in Math and a Masters degree in Psychology. But despairing of the body politic in India, he applied for an internship at a medical institution in London and some months later was invited to England. He realized, early though, *world map and given it international acclaim.*

Afghanistan's political troubles took a turn for the worse in the April 1978 coup when Afghan communists overthrew President Daoud. The regime began a revolutionary policy of modernization, but in the process alienated every segment of the Afghan people and consequently Muslim-led tribal rebellions broke out all over the country. When it was clear that the new regime had lost control, the Soviet Union invaded in December 1979 opening up yet another saga of guerrilla rebellion across the 29 provinces. Under Iranian influence, the Islamic factor grew in importance in the resistance.

But by 1988, the new Soviet leadership retracted from almost all of its Breznev-era military commitments in the Third World and in April that year signed agreements in Geneva committing to withdraw its forces from Afghanistan.

that he would not be able to travel, because the Indian government declined his request for foreign exchange.

So when, some years later as an employment officer with the Government of India, Dr. Sodhi's indulgence was sought in bribery and nepotism, he hung his boots and, this time, made a determined effort to leave India.

Dr. Sodhi says his socialist leanings made him spurn, with disgust, the hypocrisy of the elitist and the corruption in India at the time. "The feeling of powerlessness to change the pseudo systems and my extreme dissatisfaction for the way things happened in India forced my departure," he says.

Dr. Sid Sodhi and his family

Dr. Sodhi turned to Canada. He had applied to Bonneville School in Alberta in 1960 and was granted an appointment. His remuneration was to be $6,800 per year, which he thought was a good enough reason to get out of bed. He says that on June 3, 1961, he sailed on an Italian ship that took him from Bombay to Naples. He then travelled to England by train and later by sea to Montreal.

But Dr. Sodhi's assignment at Bonneville School in Alberta was to begin only in September and since he couldn't afford the holiday he applied to the department of

Even as the Soviet forces were folding up and beating a retreat home, the communist government of Dr. Najibullah continued to stay in power.

But trouble was brewing as the 16 or more Islamic parties training in Pakistan poured into Afghanistan, formed alliances and fought for reins of power.

The Mujaheedin leader Rahbani finally seized power but his reign was short lived. The Taliban ultimately wrested control from the Mujaheedin, taking Afghanistan down the road to misery.

Indeed, religious fundamentalism is Afghanistan's political ethos today. Ahmed Samin, an Afghan refugee in Canada says : "Men and women are whipped on the streets, if stringent regulations concerning the wearing of the pardah by women or the growing of a beard by the men are not obeyed.

The women, he says, are barred from schools and universities as well as from seeking

Manpower Resources with the government of Canada in Ontario. Dr. Sodhi says the recruiting officer subtly suggested that his turban (the head cover worn by Sikhs in India) and his flowing beard could scare the children at the hospital, for which the job was posted.

"His observation blew me," he says. "I cried all the way to the saloon and shaved my head and face. I had lost my identity as a Sikh. The incident depressed me. I became lonely and wanted to go back to India," he remembers.

But he didn't. Instead, he boarded a train and travelled to Bonneville School in the summer, where he taught Math and Science. He says acute loneliness often drove him to tears. It was compounded by the fact that his professional credentials were not being accepted. "We had to be tested for equivalency, the children laughed at our pronunciation, I was not invited to the Friday parties, probably because I was different." Dr. Sodhi says there was a feeling of powerlessness, great anxiety and the need to meet another East Indian," he says.

Nonetheless, behind the emotional veneer, Dr. Sodhi is made of sterner stuff. He put the hurt and injury behind him and got on with his life and went on to complete his Bachelor of Education at the University of Alberta and his Doctorate in Psychology. He retired as a Professor of Education at Dalhousie University and is currently a Registered Psychologist at Jason Roth & Associates in Halifax.

Tanzanian from India sits in Canada's parliament

Deepak Obhrai came to Canada in September 1977 from Tanzania when socialist policies were getting deep-rooted there and education and opportunities were on a decline.

work. They are chastised if their window drapes are drawn open and may venture out of their homes only with their husbands.

Just as well Afghanistan's elitist and educated chose to leave. The US consulate, Samin says, were at the time looking for educated Afghans wanting to immigrate to the United States. In those years at least 2.5 million people sought refugee status in Iran and Pakistan, while others turned to Russia and Tajekistan.

What did all this cost Afghanistan? Nearly one million dead, 535,000 disabled veterans, 700,000 widows and orphans and a refugee exodus of 5.9 million people to Pakistan, Iran and the West including one million children born in camps.

The terrorist attacks on the World Trade Centre's twin towers on September 11 got Afghanistan broiled in greater misery. The Taliban movement which rules the country refused to hand over suspected terrorist

"The children would have no future at all," he says. "So I left."

Obhrai says in response to a pointed question about nationhood, that emigrating is a monumental step which forces you to cut ties with family and friends and the environment itself. "Of course, when an environment becomes uncomfortable, you leave and do not look back. Nevertheless you cannot separate yourself from roots," he notes.

Obhrai started out in Canada from zero. "It was a tremendous upheaval, because mentally you still are back home and no progress can take place in that condition. They say it takes some 12 years for an immigrant to catch up with a Canadian-born in accessing opportunities."

Deepak Obhrai

There was always the dilemma of whether or not he had done the right thing. "There was cultural shock too – fortunately, I did some schooling in London, so I was aware of the systems."

Obhrai says that upon coming to Canada he quickly formed a friend circle and that became the support system. Then having made the contacts in Calgary, he took to community work and from thereon saw the need to take up people's causes.

"It was during Mulroney's time when

Osama Bin Laden, who is allegedly charged with masterminding the terror attacks on the US forcing a war on terrorism by the US and allies. The bombing which began on October 7, 2001 continues as this book goes to the press.

The fact is that the greater part of the misery of the third world comes not from poverty, population growth, low resource, violence or famine. The misery is rooted in illiteracy. Of course, it's a vicious cycle: A low literacy threshold upstages family planning, forces unbridled migration from villages to cities, lowers employment, breeds poverty which promotes violence, which brings misery and so on.

Having said that, the UN report on Afghanistan, which concludes that life there is hardly worth living, should come as no surprise.

With an average life expectancy of about 40 years, a staggering mortality rate of 25.7 percent for children

people were detached from public affairs, that I took the decision to plunge into politics," he says. Today, as Reform MP, I am part of the debate in parliament and can influence law making. My ethnicity encourages people to turn to me on issues affecting the immigrant community."

Obhrai says that although we in Canada are cruising along fine, there are some fundamental problems – high taxation which has eroded our standard of living – is one of them. This, he says, is compounded by the fact that because parliament is not the effective tool for change, people and organizations not elected have been given the power to voice opinion. "Canada's face has changed dramatically these last ten years but the laws have not changed to reflect that reality," he says.

Reflecting on what it means to be an immigrant, Obhrai says he has been a part of the minority all his life. "In any country there will be sections of people that are bigoted. But we must work with the broader section of society, where people are open-minded. By and large, diversity is a reality that most accept," he says.

Obhrai has faced discrimination. Citing an incident, he tells of the time when he applied for a job in Calgary, to the mechanical services department, and was refused it, despite having all the qualifications for the job. He says he wrote to the manager in protest and asked for an explanation. "After a good fight I was given the job," he says.

A few months later, the two became buddies and when Obhrai invited him over for drinks he asked him to give him a truthful answer about why he had turned down his application.

The man confessed that Obhrai was the first coloured man that came to him for a job. He said he had not met East Indians before and was therefore frightened.

under five years old, and an illiteracy rate of 64 percent, Afghanistan ranks among the most destitute, war-weary countries in the world in terms of human development, according to an analysis by the United Nations Development Programme (UNDP).

In statement released in October this year, an official at UNDP, Sakiko Fukuda-Parr, noted that Afghanistan was "worse off than almost any country in the world. The country's social and economic indicators are comparable, or lower than the indicators for Sub-Saharan Africa".

According to UNDP's annual human development index, Afghans have among the lowest life-expectancies in the world. Seventy percent of the Afghan population is estimated to be undernourished, with only 13 percent having access to improved water resources, the statement said.

What's the bottom line? The report says nearly two-thirds of Afghan adults are illiterate. Only five

Pakistani brings his talent to Canada's 5-star hospitality

On a good day, especially when the Halifax Sheraton was hosting a banquet, Tahir Salamat, the hotel's former Executive Chef would be challenged to buy a truck-load of garden fresh produce or dairy and cattle products worth anywhere up to $25,000.

What did Salamat have to bother most about? Freshness, one would have thought. But he tends to take a long shot with his observation. "Well, the challenge is about staying on top – being the leader in the hospitality industry in Atlantic Canada," he says. "It's about keeping standards high."

Keeping standards high, he says, may mean never having to fail in meeting guest expectations. Or it may mean constant staff training and more importantly staff empowerment. "It's about building good team players and being a good coach."

Taher Salamat

But you do not teach an executive chef to "suck eggs" as the saying goes. Salamat knows his onions, having come this way from the ground up in a *countries – all in Sub-Saharan Africa - of the 172 surveyed have lower literacy rates than Afghanistan. Less than one-third of children were enrolled in schools in 1999. It is the only country in the world that barred girls from attending school, it said.*

"These indicators highlight just how appalling the situation has become for Afghans," the spokeswoman for the office of the UN Coordinator, Stephanie Bunker, says. "Most Afghans barely have a life worth living at the moment."

three-year apprenticeship at the Intercontinental Hotel in Karachi where he began by, literally, chopping them.

The urge to open his career windows on the world took him across continents: first to the Holiday Inn in Copenhagen, the Tenerif Island in Spain, then back to the Sheraton in Karachi and later to the challenge of opening the Ramada in the same city as Executive Sous Chef. Onward west again, Salamat managed hospitality at the Ramada in Saudi Arabia, the Lisboa Hotel and Casino in Macau - a thousand-room facility – and finally served as Corporate Chef at Seychelles Hotels Ltd before being invited to open a deluxe resort in Qatar.

Career hopping added up to quite something, at least, exhaustive international exposure to cuisine design and hospitality management. But Salamat was looking for a haven where he could raise his children.

"Pakistan will always be in my heart," he says. "However, Canada has opportunity and prosperity."

But Canada wasn't quite a pleasant surprise initially, when he landed at Toronto in 1997. "Despite a career in hospitality that was developed and honed at the finest hotels in the world, it took me six months to land a job in Toronto," he says. "It was despairing. I was without a job, without a house of my own and a family to manage." Salamat says: "At first hotel managements appeared not to believe my resume. They wanted me to start from scratch. I was tested rigorously. I was even asked to do the 'Black Box' test."

The Black Box in the hotel industry is obviously not the box divers look for after an aircraft has crashed. It's a box of spices and condiments that a chef digs into in order to dish up a menu item.

Halifax opened up new opportunities for Salamat in Canada. But when he was asked to do the Black Box test at one of its hotels, he declined. He said he would rather scour the competition for the hotel in that time. Regardless, he got the job. Several months later and before leaving the hotel to join the Sheraton, he says he raised the culinary standards of the hotel substantially.

Salamat, until earlier this year, was managing a 30-strong team of chefs and hospitality staff.

Looking back, he says, he has no regrets. Canada has what I have always cherished. "Human dignity and values in Canada are higher than I can ever expect in Pakistan or anywhere else in the world. "I like the fact that everybody is treated equally, that nobody is victimized because of narrow perspectives.

"Canada is better than home."

Sri Lankan band set to cross international threshold

The rock/pop trio Mir is just back from Germany where it made a debut – rubbing shoulders with bands from across the world. Like it is for most bands that have trailed a blaze, the Baden Baden festival could have been Mir's stepping stone to fame. The trio comprises Asif Illyas (vocals, guitar and programming), Shebab Illyas (bass, vocals and sampling) and Adam Dowling (drums, percussion, vocals, loop sampling)

Illyas, who left his home in Sri Lanka 20 years ago and came to Canada after a brief term in England, says that it was the rock group's release of the album "Invisible Science" last year that caught the ears of the music industry and won them a record deal with Europe.

It's Canada's innovative new band, he says, and has been part of the country's music industry for about three years.

Mir has sought to be somewhat different as a pop group. "While our music is very rock, lyrically we touch on poignant concepts and musically our strains are less traditional.

We dress them up and make them more familiar for people. "Break the walls you've built around you. You're a superheronow," are the first lines of the song. "They think you're gonna come and save the world. Subatomic swarms surround you."

The chorus lines call for reflection: "There has to be an invisible science taking over you. There has to be an invisible science taking care of you."

Mir, gets its name from the Space Station. But as Illyas explains: "In Russian, it means peace within a global village.

The Mir band: (L to R) Adam, Asif and Shehab

"Although our songs are about relationships, our lyrics dwell on cultural differences and values and we hope that in listening to them people will open their eyes of the world in a different way."

While Asif and his brother Shehab are of Sri Lankan descent Adam's heritage is Irish. "You see this cultural diversity in our music," says Illyas.

"On stage we introduce several other instruments including string and the classical tabla." He says in introducing Eastern instruments such as the sitar and the tabla to the musical phrase, he is able to meld Western music with the spirit of the east.

Mir's other album "Re-humanize Me" expresses the concern that internet, instead of bringing people together may, instead, be taking people apart. "We need to meld the old with the new," says Illyas.

The lyrics are set within a relationship threshold: "No matter what they said was true. It never changed what I felt for you. You're everything I want to be. I need you to re-humanize me." With an East Coast Music Award 2001 Nomination for Best Pop/Rock Artist and a feature spot on the ECMA National televised broadcast, Illyas expects that Mir's sounds will be now heard by millions. The group's acclaimed Mir Supershow is now going to be a regular on the social calendar. The show features a night of music with special guests comprising some of Canada's finest artists with a 17 piece orchestra including members of Symphony Nova Scotia.

Illyas brushes aside any suggestion that he may have felt discriminated in Canada and that success could have eluded him on account of being a person of colour. "Firstly, I have had neither language nor cultural barriers. But more importantly, I think our parents urged us to realize that we were no different from any others.

A Muslim by birth, Illyas says religion sometimes gives people a false sense of security. "I respect religion. But I think there is a greater need to examine one's own spirit rather than the spirit behind the words written thousands of years ago. "My parents never thrust their ideas on us. That's why we don't see ourselves as different from any other."

Indian community worker says home is comfort within you

Sometime last year, Pratima Devichand alighted from the train at New Delhi and set foot on a platform teaming with humanity. Adjusting her red hat, she surged forward, making her way through the crowds, her leather boots grabbing the attention of idle men who gleefully ogled at her. She stopped at a pay phone and called a relative.

"Hire a rickshaw," he said, giving her directions to get there. "Be careful with your money and don't chat with the driver. Your Canadian accent may give you away. Remember, they've been ambushing women these days. Get here before sundown. It's not safe after that."

Pratima Devichand

Devichand says: "All that was good advice. But it left me cold with fear and anxiety. Was I really on home ground?"

Nationhood, some say, is an accident of birth. Roots may be emotional wires connecting with home. But as Devichand just discovered for herself, home is that comfort zone you create inside you. So what are roots?

A few months ago, Devichand pieced together "My Journey Continues", a radio story that was aired on CBC's Outfront program. The story is about Devichand's journey home to India, to roots, where she discovered sadly, she did not belong.

Devichand travelled to Kulu in Simla, to green valleys and snow-clad mountains and to her father's home after many years. "Kulu brought back memories, but everything I saw, I saw through rose coloured glasses. It was not home."

She says: "My people told me to slow down, change my body language, stroll along looking feminine and not to stride purposefully. They said she should treat people according to their social classes. "Do not pick up the dishes from the table. Do not be straightforward. That will be interpreted as being rude," they said.

Devichand says all this brought in much confusion within her. In stores, where she shopped, her unpracticed Hindustani stood out embarrassingly. Her family kin translated conversations for her. "The men stared at me –it's common for men to blatantly stare at women in India - and all this awakened in me this confused notion about home."

What Devichand is saying is that while she once felt she did not belong in Canada because of a foreign culture and outlook, she now realizes that she neither feels a sense of belonging in India. "Home is not in the land, but perhaps inside you. It's an imaginary homeland," she says.

Devichand, who moved to Canada at 15, after a brief stay in England, has completed a Masters in Community Health and Epidemiology at Dalhousie, after obtaining an undergraduate degree in microbiology and international development.

Her work in health, of course, looks beyond the physical state and into those mental spaces that people find themselves in, fighting a struggle, as some immigrants do.

A couple of years ago, Devichand was also involved in a program that required her to create and organize a network of health interpreters who would be available to patients and doctors as the need arose. Now she's pursuing a career in film.

Devichand left India as a young girl and moved to England. She says, the transition was more difficult than it was in Canada. "My peers at school hung out in cliques and I had to find a place among those cliques which was not very easy."

But as she says, with home lying somewhere within her, the journey continues.

Indian activist seeks broader opportunity base for newcomers

Ratna Omidvar met her Iranian-born husband in Germany in 1974, but travelled to Iran in order to start a new life there.

By 1979 Iran's revolution was in its throes and there was this sense of excitement - of a new dawn of democracy unfolding, she says. "Unfortunately this did not quite take place as we had hoped. In 1981 when the war with Iraq broke out, we decided to leave Iran - and very quickly - in order to escape any involvement in it".

The Omidvars managed to cross the border into Turkey right at the time when a coup was in the making there. Omidvar says they later travelled to Germany and temporarily settled down there. But it was not home.

The search for one meant that America had to be ruled out. "The rabid anti-Moslem, anti-Iranian sentiment in the US would not make us welcome," she says. "We were looking for a gentler, kinder country, prosperous, but not embroiled in war. The absence of Canada from the stage of the powerful was of significance to us. When you see your life go away in a night, you pretty much know what you want thereafter," she observes.

"But settlement was deadly," says Omidvar. "Things just did not fall in place. Canada was going through a huge recession at the time and I experienced my first brush with racism. I was refused access to an apartment because I was brown. The search for an apartment, for a job, for child care – all of that forced us into a

Ratna Omidvar

state of depression, she says. "Overall, we went through five years of teething problems, until things eased up a bit."

Omidvar says that her husband went through those motions too. An engineer by training, he failed to obtain work and so took up a cleaning job at a superstore. But things have changed today. He has been gainfully employed as a design engineer for the last ten years and she serves as executive director of The Maytree Foundation which is getting Ottawa to focus on factors affecting immigrants and refugees in Canada.

How does she feel about nationhood today? Omidvar says: "I don't think one can underestimate the feelings of loyalty and commitment that new citizens bring, especially when Canada throws a life line to them. If it were not for the chance that Canada so generously gave us, I don't honestly know what we would be doing.

"Because I owe so much to Canada, I am incredibly passionate about retaining and strengthening one of the world's greatest democracies. That is also why we feel so dismayed and puzzled about Quebec." But Omidvar is quick to make the distinction. "This loyalty and passion for Canada, however, in no way takes away from me the feelings for India. India will always be a very strong part of me, but Canada is my future."

The Maytree Foundation, Omidvar says, is currently working on issues of access to trades and professions. "I do not think that we can continue to do well by Canada and by immigrants if we don't live up to the implicit or explicit promises we make them," she says. " I am working on developing a framework that can be adopted by stakeholders such as government, regulators and employers.

In her keynote address at the National Settlement Conference in Kingston, Ontario on June 18 this year, Omidvar made some pertinent observations. The timing for the conference, she said, could not have been better. "The world around us is moving at a dizzy pace. The flow of knowledge, information, goods and people has changed the context and environment in many areas, including immigration. But somehow, we don't seem to be doing well with immigration."

She was making the point that the image of a lawyer or doctor driving a taxi is almost burnt into our national consciousness and that the indisputable co-relation between race and poverty should be a grave concern for all Canadians.

Settlement, she says, cannot end at speaking basic English. It should mean speaking enough English to sit around a board room. "If the real test of settlement is not language skills but active participation in our democratic institutions, then we have to examine the capacity and ability of Canada to successfully facilitate that participation," she says.

Pakistani businessman owns chain of nursing, retirement homes

They say you must never deprive someone of hope: it might be all they have.

Indeed, hope was all that Munawar Hussain clung to when his father left India in the post-partition years to settle down in Pakistan. "That was economic disaster for the family. It happened as I was dreaming dreams in my youth. There was this restlessness within me to change destiny's hand," he says. "I wanted to leave home."

Hussain and his wife Gloria

But Hussain's father would not let him. At the time, conservative thinking in the Indian subcontinent about Western social conduct was very normal and Hussain's ambitions had to be crushed for a while. Not for long- Hussain stood his ground and with some money loaned to him by his brother he got his father to say "yes" and boarded a bus to Quetta and ultimately took the long road to Germany.

At the time, Hussain had hoped to study medicine. But after two years in Munich studying German, he realized he could not pay for his medical studies. Hussain knows that there is no elevator to success... you have to take the stairs. That's exactly what he did. He abandoned Germany, drew on his experience as a tabulating machine operator in Pakistan and qualified for immigration to Canada.

Pierre Trudeau's open door policy at the time had opened the flood gates to immigration from Asia, the qualifying criteria shifting from race to skills.

But as Hussain observes, only the professional elite of Asian countries came to Canada at the time. "Thus one saw only a handful of Indians or Pakistanis on the streets of Toronto. It was a kind of culture shock."

Of course there is a sea-change in that landscape today, where 40 per cent of high school students are foreign born and police departments are scrambling to keep up with their changing communities.

Hussain got a foot in the door of McLellan Stewart in Toronto, starting out initially as a tabulating machine operator, oblivious of what the future would hold for him. It was in Toronto that he met Gloria, his wife, who is more than only mother to his three children.

They say, rightly or wrongly, behind every successful man, is a woman. Gloria, who was a senior nurse at the blood bank in Toronto Western at the time, spurred Hussain to greater things. They ultimately left their jobs to buy out Groves Park Lodge in Ontario.

"Our first flirtation with business saw us mired in a $3 million investment venture in which we poured all of our savings of about $300,000," says Hussain. But the deal did not go through. Hussain says the former owners of the lodge wanted back wages, the Canadian Union of Employees would not let the deal go through. About $100,000 was stuck in the spokes of a legal wrangle, so to say.

But life's about falling, rising and getting on with it again. So today, Hussain, who is Chairman of the Board of Gem Healthcare Group owns a chain of nursing and retirement homes, real estate properties and travel accommodations in Canada and the United States, many of them in Halifax, Truro, Amherst and Ontario.

The Group cumulatively provides thousands of room nights a year in over ten facilities and employs hundreds of people. The better known among them are Melville Heights and the Garden Inn in Halifax, the Centennial Villa in Amherst and the Groves Park Lodge in Ontario.

Away from corporate success, Hussain is trying to make a difference in the community as well. He is chairman of the Nova Scotia Islamic Community Centre and is spearheading the work on the building of a new Mosque at Kearney Lake in Halifax.

Was Hussain a victim of bigotry on the road to success. "The discrimination of people exists in my home country as it does everywhere else," he says. "Canada is the best place in the world to live. I wouldn't bother about bigotry."

Conservative Asian communities have traditionally resisted the temptation to raise children in the West. But Hussain holds a different view. "I don't contribute to that mindset. You can live in any environment under the hospice of Islam and accommodate other beliefs. You do not have to change, but you must learn to understand the other side as well," he observes.

"It's not for us to judge. "Only the individual soul decides right from wrong."

Indian film maker does not take success seriously

Deepa Mehta   Photo courtesy Zeitgeist Films

Deepa Mehta, Canada's famous film-maker, has poignantly told her story since coming to Canada in the film *Sam and Me*. It's a film set in Canada and is about male, white collar immigrants. She says she considers *Sam and Me* among her best films because "it reflects to a large extent my Canadian experience. The desire to belong and realizing that however sappy it sounds, home is within you."

Emigrating is difficult, she says alluding to V.S. Naipaul's book "The Enigma of Arrival" in which he writes: "We never really leave home and we never really arrive." Mehta thinks this is true for her as a first generation immigrant.

She came to Canada not for the reasons most immigrants present. "I wouldn't have left India if I hadn't fallen in love with a Canadian, and followed him to his home like a good wife," she says. "Living in India , I never thought there was any reason to leave home. My roots are set deeply in India, it's culture, its smells, it's colour and it's ethos. While however much I love Canada, I still feel like its adopted child."

Despite the fact that Mehta is well-known as a film maker, she has to grapple with the challenges of getting the finances together. "We are a very young industry here and it will take time to build our own star system and have faith in our own stories, multicultural or otherwise," she says.

Mehta says success has taught her not to take it seriously. "She's a hard and unpredictable mistress," she observes. Just as well she makes no predictions of where a successful film maker should see herself ten years down the road.

She leaves you thinking when she says "Canada evokes much affection within me, but never passion. Commenting on her own impressions of whether or not Canadians appreciate a diverse society, she says: "I don't know...

probably not. When you don't understand you just assume. And this works specifically when people don't take the time to understand folks who are different from them. "

But quoting Pico Iyer's observations in his lecture from 'Outsiders hope for a Global Future', she says she believes one must challenge oneself to imagine Canada as a 'space between'. "That space is one that cannot be labeled and is vibrant, subtle and imaginative."

Indian community worker says racism is two-way street

Racism is a two-way street. It's not, as it is made out to be, a white man's sole "culpa." Faisal Samad has come to understand that "reverse racism" in our communities is not even subtle. It kicks you in the shin.

India -born, Samad came to Halifax for his tertiary education, after initial schooling in Saudi Arabia. The options, as he says, were few. "The Middle East was out of the question and my future in India, my father thought, was limited."

Today he is a YMCA support worker. He began working for the organization's outreach program in its fledgling stage at Halifax West High School. It's an outreach program in schools, whose goals are to bridge the gaps between cultures and breakdown the barriers that come in the way of settlement and integration.

"When I first started work for the progam at Halifax West, its staff were hardly accustomed to dealing with newcomers," Samad says. "There was absolutely no cultural sensitivity. Arabs were seen as a threat. I've heard those racist remarks thrown at them: go back to your country, why are you here."

> ***"I had to explain to mainstream Canadians that the 'hijab' was not to conceal baldness but to practice modesty....that fasting during Ramadan was not to hurt oneself, but to come closer to God. We had to show them similarities with Lenten fasting and the similarities in the worship by Christians, Jews and Muslims."***

Samad says the friction often built up so much as to kick up inter-racial fights at soccer games. The Arab girls who wore the "*hijab*" would arouse suspicion among white kids. His job at the time was to create understanding. "I had to explain to mainstream Canadians that the *hijab* was not to conceal baldness but to practice modesty....that fasting during Ramadan was not to hurt oneself, but to come closer to God. We had to show them similarities with Lenten fasting and the similarities in the worship by Christians, Jews and Muslims," he says.

A lot has been said about all this perhaps, but the point Faisal makes is that today diversity in schools in not so much a challenge – although the YMCA outreach program has expanded so greatly as to be present in at least 15 schools in Metro.

A third of the thousand or more students at the erstwhile Halifax West High School were of ethnic origin, making it then the most multicultural school east of Montreal.

"A great deal has changed. School managements today bend over backwards to help newcomers. Even inclusive curriculum is taking shape," he says.

But while Samad sounds a positive note there, he recognizes the fact that racism is a two-way street. He says he has seen white and black kids feel discriminated by Arabs.

"The rich Arab kids party a lot, some are loud and all this tends to intimidate white kids. I've heard Arab youth make racist passes at white girls and have seen fights result from that distaste."

Faisal has intervened sometimes. He says he has rebuked youth about their value systems. "I have had to tell them that if they would not violate a Muslim girl, why should they violate a non-Muslim girl. They had to be told that parking one's car in the middle of the street is crude arrogance.

"I once confronted an Arab and told him that by virtue of employing an Indian cook in his home country he could not take away the dignity of all Indians. "

But while Samad sounds a positive note there, he recognizes the fact that racism is a two-way street. He says he has seen white and black kids feel discriminated by Arabs.

Samad believes that Canada is a fair and just country, that it's free, for as long as you do not abuse freedom, and that racism is only about ignorance.

But what the YMCA outreach program has done to broaden cross-cultural understanding in schools, a similar catalyst can do to deal with diversity in the public or corporate sectors.

One place, Faisal would like to see this happen, is in law enforcement. "Law enforcement needs to be more diverse in order to reflect the changing demographics of our province and it ought to be more culturally-sensitive, anyway," he says.

Afghan engineer says religious fundamentalism is his country's ethos

In the years following the military occupation of Afghanistan by Soviet forces, neighbouring Pakistan and Iran had opened their doors to the one dominant Islamic party at the time in the country, which it later fragmented. The Afghan Mujaheedin finally established a base in Pakistan where it trained in warfare, says Ahmed Samin, a young engineer who left the war-torn country some years later for more peaceful terrains.

In 1989, although the Soviet forces had folded up and were beating a retreat home, the communist government of Dr. Najibullah continued to stay in power. But trouble was brewing as the 16 or more Islamic parties training in Pakistan poured into Afghanistan, formed alliances and fought for reins of power.

"The Mujaheedin leader Rahbani finally seized power," Samin says. But that was short lived. "The Taliban ultimately wrested control from the Mujaheedin, taking Afghanistan down the road to misery," he says.

Religious fundamentalism, Samin says is Afghanistan's political ethos today. "Men and women are whipped on the streets, if stringent regulations concerning the wearing of the *pardah* by women or the growing of a beard by the men are not strictly observed. The women, Samin says, are barred from schools and universities as well as from seeking work. They are chastised if their window drapes are drawn open and cannot venture out of their homes without their husbands.

Ahmed Samin with his family in Canada

About that time, the country's elitist and educated chose to leave. The US consulate, Samin says, were looking for educated Afghans wanting to immigrate to the United States. In those years at least 2.5 million people sought refugee status in Iran and Pakistan, while others turned to Russia and Tajekistan.

Samin had studied engineering in Afghanistan, but when it was time to leave, he turned to Iran first, because of language and cultural familiarity. He later travelled to India where he wrote against the political tide in Afghanistan in Persian weeklies.

He was granted landed immigrant status in Canada on humanitarian grounds. But like most newcomers, Samin soon realized that he could not be employed as an engineer. He had first to register with APENS (Association of Professional Engineers of Nova Scotia). Samin was willing, although he got to know later the process of getting licensed as an engineer is a long-drawn one. The University at which he studied was not listed on the APENS "Black Book". That meant he would have to submit transcripts, course descriptions and translations to the licensing authority and finally sit for examinations.

"Not a problem," he says. "I shall go through the process and requalify." He currently works as a storekeeper to make a living.

But Samin has learnt the virtues of tolerance, not just tolerance for the way systems work, but tolerance in the journey of life. Putting aside his career as an engineer, Samin has trained as a cultural health interpreter and is qualified to help newcomers in the health sector. He extends that tolerance to religion. "In my travels to India and Iran, I have visited mosques, mandirs (Hindu temples) and churches and have prayed with the same devotion," he says.

Most importantly, he counts his blessings by the flowers that bloom not by the leaves that fall. "I've come to Canada from a war-torn country. Naturally, I enjoy the peace here," he says.

Businessman leaves homeland - has distaste for its Islamic fundamentalism

Sohail (Mike) Ansari is doing for Nova Scotia what a government ought to be doing. He is bringing money into the province from other parts of the world to finance local projects.

"There is a lot of money outside banking...there are private investors and venture capitalists looking for projects that can hit the ground running," he says. "I think I know what lenders are looking for and that's how I put packages together, essentially putting money where the mouth is." Ansari identifies projects with promise and lures an investor to put up the money. In doing so, he's spurring business and growing the economy. Unfortunately, as Ansari says, lenders look for big bucks and do not look at projects where the financing portfolio is short of a million.

Ansari has been putting together finance packages even to extricate companies out of receivership. He says early this year he was bringing in close to $100 million from other parts of the world into the province. His work takes him to other provinces, sometimes even to meet with fishermen and farmers and work out financial solutions to agricultural projects.

Ansari has been a banker for about 23 years, some of those years spent on home ground in Pakistan and the rest in the United Kingdom as well as Saudi Arabia and Bahrain – the oil-rich, tax-free havens in the Persian Gulf. But the Sohails moved to Canada with their children a couple of years ago to "set their minds free."

Mike Sohail Ansari

A Muslim by birth, Ansari says he adopted Canada as his new home to free himself from Islamic fundamentalism in Pakistan. "That country is a hotbed of religious fundamentalism. The Press is free today, but that freedom is gone tomorrow," he says. He feels he needs the freedom of thought, faith and speech. "I don't want my kids to be subjected to this bigotry or to be forced into believing that theirs is the only true religion and that they may even kill to defend the faith."

Ansari says he wants his children to decide the faith they must practice and has moved to Canada to be allowed the freedom to do that.

"Uprooting ourselves was no problem," says Naheed, his wife. "The children had a Western education in Bahrain, anyway." She also admits she has no problems with life in Canada. "The children were brought up to discern right from wrong," she says.

A Physics and Math teacher in Pakistan and Bahrain, Naheed preferred to set up residence in Halifax because "it's a peaceful city to bring up children." But Naheed does not teach. Rather than go through the process in order to be teacher-certified in Canada, she chose to buy into a business. Some time ago, she invested $40,000 initially to set up International News at Scotia Mall.

Although Mike and Naheed came here for different reasons, I think what they cherish most is freedom.

Pakistani pilot is proud to fly for Canada

Those who knew Abdul Qayyum Gill, must have, at sometime, wondered what's a jet fighter pilot doing managing a grocery store. The ordinary conclusion would have been that Gill must re-qualify. But Gill, who ran Iqbals' Grocery on Robie street in Halifax and who will now fly for Canada, brushes aside any suggestion that Canada's air force took nine years to recognize his credentials.

"It took three months," he says. "But becoming a Canadian citizen which is mandatory for that job took me five years."

Gill is now set to fly behind the controls of a CF-18 fighter, having been accepted as a skilled pilot. "This is quite the jet aircraft I was trained to fly," he says. Gill trained as a fighter pilot in Pakistan's air force and served as a pilot and instructor for 16 years at the controls of Pakistan's fighter jets and jet interceptors including F-16 and Mirage fighters and MiG jets.

When retirement was around the bend, Gill was looking at the future with some gloom. "For as long as you're in the air force, you hold much prestige. But once you're out, modest pensions do not allow you to maintain the same lifestyle," he says. Gill was also thinking about a good education and future for his children. Canada became an automatic choice.

But having made a landing, Gill actually wondered if he would regain his wings once again. He thought his age would be a barrier. But Iqbals's grocery was a good networking outlet. "I met with Canadians who were of great help. One of them told me age is not a barrier – if it was it would be discriminatory.

I took heart and qualified for the Canadian Airline Transport

Abdul Qayyum Gill: dual citizenship, dual loyalties

Pilot License," he explains. In the process, Gill did 800 flying hours in Canada.

Before being accepted as a fighter pilot in the Canadian air force, he did ground examinations and flight tests on multiengine VFRs and tests for instrument ratings and graduated from the Canadian Forces leadership and recruit school in Quebec.

So now Gill will be going places. He has, initially, been assigned to Moose Jaw – the air force base in Saskatchewan and will probably be commissioned as an Instructor Pilot for Hawks – the jets he has flown all his life.

The question about loyalties to nationhood is automatic. What would he do if he was to fly sorties into Pakistan for the Canadian air force. Gills says he has dual citizenship and therefore dual loyalties. "Canada, anyway, deploys its forces for peacekeeping and not for aggression. If I am deployed to keep the peace in Pakistan, I surely will do my duties," he says.

Even while managing Iqbal's Grocery, Gill was happy to be in Canada. "Growing up children are parents' business. Of course, there must have been peer pressure, but while we trained our children to live in a modern society, we exhorted them to stick to their own sense of values." In the process, he says, not once did he or the family experience discrimination. Gill and his wife, Ghazala, have two children, a son, Zariyan, 13, and a daughter, Neriman, 12.

"I have been helped so much by white Canadians - well beyond their call of duty," he says.

Gill tells of how Mardy Plumstead, the top boss of Transport Canada in the Atlantic region actually flew out of Moncton and showed up at his store to hand him the admission criteria. "Later he even got his instructors to fly on weekends only to accommodate my working schedules," he says.

Prior to joining the Canadian air force, Gill was made job offers by air forces in the Middle East – where he would have been commissioned as a civilian instructor. "But I preferred to fly for Canada because it's what makes me proudest," he says.

Emigration out of Europe

West European emigration in the twentieth century

The Great Depression of the 1930s succeeded in choking off almost all immigration to Canada. During these years of economic devastation and widespread unemployment, the federal government strove hard to seal off Canada not only to prospective immigrants but also to refugees fleeing Nazi Germany, particularly Jewish refugees. There can be no doubt that Ottawa's restrictive legislation reflected the general Canadian attitude towards immigration, for Canadians across the country took the view that immigrants threatened scarce jobs in an economy that in 1933 saw almost one-quarter of the labour force unemployed.

Among those barred from entering

Holocaust survivor speaks for the millions who cannot

Philip Riteman's prisoner number identification tattooed on his forearm in the concentration camps of Auschwitz during Hitler's horrifying holocaust is an everyday reminder to him of what hate can do. "If Hitler was not stopped, there would be no coloured people in the world, and the rest of would be slaves," he says. Riteman was commenting on the seriousness of Hitler's resolve to give the world a pure Aryan race.

Riteman was only 13 years old when German soldiers invaded his hometown on the Polish-Russian border and took them to a ghetto teeming with some 35,000 people. Six months later they were put on trains and taken to Auschwitz. When after a seven-day journey, the

Phillip Riteman

train pulled up at Auschwitz station, German soldiers wielding bayonets dispersed the family and in a flash, Riteman saw his father and mother, five brothers, two sisters, nine uncles and aunts and his grandparents sent to their death.

"On that station, I saw German soldiers take babies from their mother's arms and rip them limb by limb," he says, fighting back tears. Riteman was put to hard labour in the Auschwitz, Birkeman and Dachau camps, building crematoriums where at least 20,000 people were being burnt everyday over day and night shifts. "I've seen rows of women stripped naked preparing to be burnt with their children. I've seen daily executions of men and even pregnant women and young girls. I've seen men dig their graves. I've seen piles and piles of bones in the camps. "The Nazis would take us to the pile of bones, make us tie them up with ropes and then burn them.

Riteman, sometimes weeping as he speaks, tells of how he was whipped everyday while carrying sand and bricks to build those crematoriums. "Fefluckte, they would say and whip us." (Fefluckte is the German word for the "f" expletive). He shows off his crushed thumb that was jammed at the hinge of a door by a German soldier and a bruised neck hit by a flying bullet. He looks at the photos of bunks at the barracks where he slept on plain board huddled with other prisoners in those years and recalls the time when he worked on a farm and lived on oats given to the horses. He says he even survived the "Death March" when prisoners unable to walk anymore were brutally shot by German soldiers

Riteman finally saw that light at the end of the tunnel four years later one morning. On the horizon he saw soldiers of another kind coming towards the barracks on their stomachs He looked around and in gaping anticipation realized that the German trucks and tanks had been abandoned. "These were the Americans. They set us free. Our veterans, whether they be Americans, Canadians, or Russians are the only heroes I know," he says. "They saved the

Canada during the1930s were thousands of desperate refugees. The persecution of the Jews was particularly savage, especially after the German invasion of Austria in March 1938. Thousands of the Jews who managed to escape Nazi brutality, mainly from Poland and Hungary sought refuge in Canada, but by and large their appeals were ignored. Anti-Semitism was rife throughout Canada, where, in some places, Jews could not hold particular jobs, own property, or stay in certain hotels. It was most strident in Quebec.

At the base of German immigration to Canada were those brave men and women who travelled across the Atlantic from Europe to colonial Halifax in September 1750 on the ship Anne. Among those thousands of passengers invariably were new settlers for Nova Scotia. One such immigrant who obtained his naturalization papers on May 16, 1871 in Halifax was

Filehne in Prussia. He quickly established himself as a tobacconist in the downtown Halifax.

Henry Busch of Hamburg left his mark on Nova Scotia's landscape as a noted architect. The Halifax Academy Building is one of the examples of second empire buildings designed by Busch.

But it was in the aftermath of the Second World War that a new wave of German immigrants arrived in Canada.

Halifax as the major eastern railway terminus was the favoured port for immigrant vessels and it was from here that newcomers could travel by rail to western Canada .

Furthermore the basis for the renewed presence of the Jewish community came through migration from Germany and adjoining territories.

Between the wars, 97,000 German-speaking immigrants came to Canada from Poland, Austria, Czechoslovakia, and Germany.

world."

When the war ended, Riteman lived in a DP (Displaced Persons) camp, where American soldiers and Red Cross personnel were compiling family history of holocaust survivors. These notes were published in North American newspapers and that's how two of Riteman's aunts, one in Montreal and the other in Newfoundland were able to establish contact with him.

The aunt in Montreal failed to convince the government in Ottawa of the need to bring Riteman to Canada. But Newfoundland, which was not part of the Confederation at the time, welcomed him in 1946.

Today at 76 he still manages a rug trading business in Bedford, Nova Scotia but spends the greater part of the day speaking about the lessons of the holocaust to students at schools, as well as at churches and universities. "I speak for the millions who cannot.

When I speak to German children, I see them cry and I tell them they have every reason to feel proud of their country today. But I tell them, too, of the evil that hate can generate. "I grew up learning never to harm anyone. We believed in the Ten Commandments. But when I came to Auschwitz I said never mind God, where is humanity," he says. "I tell children, if you see evil, stand up against it."

"I grew up learning never to harm anyone. We believed in the Ten Commandments. But when I came to Auschwitz I said never mind God, where is humanity," he says. "I tell children, if you see evil, stand up against it."

Farmers and agricultural workers settled in the vicinity of older German settlements on the Prairies. A smaller number of artisans, labourers, and shopkeepers moved on to British Columbia.

The arrivals included many German-speaking refugees from Romania, Yugoslavia, and the former Austria-Hungary.

When the German troops retreated from Romania, the Russians occupied Bucharest and by 1946 the communist takeover was complete forcing an exodus of refugees out of Romania.

Later, when the ban on immigration of German nationals was lifted in 1950, the number of Germans entering the country increased dramatically to about a quarter of a million by 1961.

The 1996 Canadian census recorded the presence of 2,757,140 people of German descent living in Canada.

Among the German scientists of distinction, is Gerhard

British photographer says Canada is a culture shock

You would think that a British citizen would take to Canada like a duck to water. But you'll be surprised, says June Spindloe, who came to Canada from England five years ago.

"It's truly a culture shock for us, for many reasons," she explains. "Firstly, because the British are arrogant, the courtesy of Canadian society appears to be overwhelming. How does one respond to a parcel pick-up suggestion at a store in Canada when one is used to jostling at crammed supermarkets in Britain?

Spindloe's point is that while many would think British and Canadian cultures and lifestyles are akin, they are really not. "The Tim Horton's coffee culture that let's you walk out with a cup is a world apart from England's, where you must sit down for a cup of coffee.

Spindloe trained as a photographer in England but works as a cosmetician at Sears where she promotes the brand Shishedo. That is a Japanese brand of toiletries and cosmetics and which is why

June Spindloe

Herzberg, a physicist, who was awarded the Nobel Prize in 1971.

In public life, at least two of the Fathers of Confederation – Charles Fisher of Fredericton and William Henry Steeves of Saint John – were of German origin.

The Right Honourable John G. Diefenbaker, of mixed German and Scottish descent, was Prime Minister of Canada from 1957 to 1963.

As well, the Right Honourable Edward Schreyer was to serve as Canada's Governor General from 1979 to 1984.

The Canadian government, during Sifton's tenure sought to limit the immigration of Italians, who he thought were illfitted for enterprise.

Most were peasants or farmers, small landowners, and rural day labourers from the impoverished south.

From among those who arrived in Canada, thousands went to work to build Canada's railways. Others worked in mines

her job actually brings her in contact with people of diverse origins – especially the Japanese, Chinese and Koreans. She says she enjoys this interaction with inter-races and therefore mixes business with pleasure. Her home is listed as a host family in the Saint Mary's University (SMU) student exchange program.

In quite the same way, she is also currently familiarizing Britons with life in Canada. Spindloe is a correspondent for the British tabloid *Canada News*. But why are Britons coming to Canada, anyway?

Spindloe thinks it's because the average Briton is struggling with low incomes, the lack of housing, high crime and stressful living. "Women are discriminated against," she says. "The fact that age, sex and marital status can influence the decision of the employer to hire or not is disconcerting."

Equally disconcerting is the class system, she says. She talks of the fact that factors about where you were born and raised, the "somewhere accent" and even religious discrimination come into play in British society. Thus the need for the average Briton to look for opportunity and a new society in Canada.

Spindloe says the Britons who come to Canada imagine that settling down will be a cakewalk. "But that's not reality. When you come here, you find you're a non-person. No credit card for six months, no house mortgage because one lacks a local credit record." She says that this is something the average Briton cannot accept. That's when the notion of an immigrant takes on a new meaning. "The immigrant syndrome is not confined only to those who speak another language," she says.

Spindloe does a hard day's work in Canada, but never dreams of getting back to Britain. "I shall never be able to resettle in Britain or fit into that class-driven society again."

where demand for labour was very high.

Some 3,000 Italians arrived in Montréal in 1904, and two years later, when construction of the trunk lines of the Grand Trunk Pacific railways began in earnest, there was a further dramatic increase in the numbers of Italians coming to Canada.

Russian settlement in Canada began in the nineteenth century when the Doukobors - a Christian peasant sect, persecuted and harassed by the Tzarist authorities fled their homelands.

According to many accounts, it was Leo Tolstoy, the famous Russian novelist who used his fame to help the Doukobors emigrate.

The first batch arrived in the 1890s and settled in the Prince Albert and Yorktown areas of Saskatchewan.

In the Ukraine, at the time, changing conditions had threatened the peace and prosperity of the Mennonites and as a result

Young Greek girl braves journey on a boat to Halifax

When World War 11 ended, European economies were in shambles and in Greece the downturn in the economy saw people out of jobs, rising inflation and a run on commodities. Kiki Katsepontes lost her father soon after. She had to cut short her education because there wasn't the means to pay for it. But the young girl had the will. "At the time people were leaving Greece by the thousands and Canada had opened its doors. So I left home as a young girl and braved a twelve-day journey on a boat destined for Nova Scotia," she says.

Peter and Kiki at the family dinner table

She walked through Pier 21's doors on New Year's Day, 1957. She remembers stepping on shore with a very ecstatic feeling laced with the determination to turn one's life around. "There were two major barriers to surmount: the weather and the language. I knew that determination changes things."

Kiki disembarked at Pier 21 and initially lived with her uncle. But what she remembers most are moments shared with a Canadian *a third of the Russian Mennonites emigrated.*

But the Doukhobors resisted compliance with the state. They refused to take the oath of allegiance, register births and marriages and neither would they allow their children to be educated in the public system.

These were widened by the actions of an extremist group, the Sons of Freedom, who liberated cattle, burnt property, and refused to till the land.

By 1911, the number of Ukrainians in Saskatchewan had declined because some Dukhobors lost their land after refusing to comply with the interpretation of the Dominion Lands Act.

Order was finally restored by the Doukhobors' spiritual leader Peter Veregin who organized them into farming communities in British Columbia where some had moved.

The 1921 census reported the presence of 100,000 people of Russian origin in Canada.

Immigration

family. "They were so overwhelmingly kind. Then a year later, Peter joined me and we got married. Life was an uphill exercise. There were sacrifices to be made."

Peter and Kiki Kantsepontes, ran a Corner store with help from their three children. That store later expanded to include a restaurant and pizzeria. It was a family-run business with the children Nicholas, Leon and Athena pitching in. The restaurant "Euro" today runs itself as the Katsepontes sit back and reflect on life.

Kiki estimates that there could have been a thousand Greek families that passed through Pier 21. Many came, but few stayed back in Halifax. Many left for upper Canada, some of whom the couple stumbled into while touring other Canadian cities. "In those days my mother and I, who were sometimes lonely, looked up the boat arrival schedules regularly and would go to Pier 21 to receive Greek families," she recalls. "Then we would bring them home and cook them a meal before we saw them off." There are probably about 200 Greek families in Nova Scotia today, many in the property business.

Three years ago when the Katsepontes went home to Greece on holiday, Bill Theodorakasso ran up to them in the street and gave them a bear's hug. When he had arrived at Pier 21 many years ago, he was kept in detention by immigration officials because he was not able to convince them in English about why his children whose names were listed on his passport were not on the boat with him. They suspected that Theodorakasso had thrown them off the boat. When in detention, Theodorakasso called Peter Katsepontes . He told him that his children were not allowed to board at Athens because they were suffering from a virus. Katsepontes translated for Theordorakasso and had him released him from detention.

was later halted by the Russian Revolution of 1917 and the Russian civil war which broke out soon after.

Russian immigrants of the post-war period represented a broader movement of professionals who integrated with relative ease. Among them were academics and physicians who acquired eminence in Canada.

According to the recent census, there were a total of 272,325 people of Russian origin in Canada in 1996

By all accounts, the first recorded Greek presence in North America is that of Juan Da Fuca or Yannis Phokas, a Greek mariner who surveyed the British Columbia coast in 1592 in the service of the Spanish monarch. But it was not until the nineteenth century when Canada's railways lines were being developed that significant Greek emigration to Canada began. By 1931, almost 10,000 Greeks had settled in Canada, mostly in Montreal and Toronto.

But Greece

Kiki and Peter have many memories to share. Having retired from active life, she now volunteers at St. George's Greek Orthodox Church on Purcell's Cove Road. The church is central to the life of the Greek community. "The church is our culture, our language, our religion and our country," she says. "That is why we, as Greeks, have not lost our identity," says Kiki. The community keeps a pulse on Greece through the country's national papers as well as through Greek television channels. The church is also catalytic in two major community celebrations in Nova Scotia - the commemoration of national day on March 25 which celebrates Greece's independence from the Turks and the annual Greek Festival.

Polish lecturer leaves with a sense of curiosity

Merek Jagelski came to Canada from Poland out of a sense of curiosity. But it's precisely that curiosity that has enabled him piece together the *Cultural Competence Handbook*. It's an essential guide for anyone who realizes the need to develop a framework of reference when dealing with people from different cultures.

Jagelski was a lecturer in Poland before he travelled to the US and finally came to Canada to study education at Mount Alison University. He says he has always wanted to test how people's identities affect them and how dual identities impact on personal growth. He currently works as the Volunteer Services Unit Manager at the Metropolitan Immigrant Settlement Association (MISA) in Halifax.

In the process of his research, Jagelski

went through a period of turmoil in the Forties. In 1940 Italian Fascists under Musolini attacked it through Alb year later the German Nazis over-ran it and remained there until 1944. Thus, by around 1950, hundreds of Greeks who could get out, left their homeland for Australia, the US and Canada.

Later, ongoing poverty and a series of repressive military dictatorships dug in.

Greece's interference in Cyprus caused Turkey to invade the island in 1974 and war almost broke out between Greece and Turkey.

It was then that Greek immigration peaked - the vast majority came to work in factories, restaurants, and maintenance. By 1996 the census reported 203,000 Greeks in Canada.

Greeks have tended to settle in large cities. The large settlements in Montreal and Toronto have resulted in concentrations of small businesses such

figured that if Canada must truly grow as a multicultural nation, then new and mainstream Canadians would have to develop a mindset or a set of skills to become truly interculturally competent in the workplace.

He makes this observation based on the feeling that Canadians must be aware of the fact that there are many different ways of living, speaking, learning, worshipping and doing business.

Merek Jageilski

In a chapter on cultural frames of reference, he notes that because culture has a critical influence on the beliefs and identities of all people, individuals can never escape their own culturally influenced identity.

Making a point about East-West characteristics of identity, he says that whereas individualism dominates the Western concept of personal identity, in Eastern cultures, the umbrella of the family converges on the individual identity.

His book makes several observations of the belief systems: the humility and self deprication characteristic of the Hindus; the concept of "hiya" which means shame - key to the Filipino character; the Chinese moral code designed to propel social harmony; religion and fate influencing the minds of the Arab people.

as "kafenions" or coffee shops which bring the community together.

Indeed, the Orthodox Church is quite at the heart of all that is Greek in spirit. As one Greek resident in Halifax observes: "The Church is our religion, our culture, our language and our country" There are, at least, 40 Greek parishes in Canada.

Greeks have taken a spot in public life as well. In 1999 Toronto had five individuals of Greek descent on City Council. In Quebec, Greek heritage candidates from the NDP, Liberals, and Conservatives have attempted to win seats in the Quebec legislature.

At the federal level Eleni Bakopanos, a Liberal from Montreal, has served in the last two Chrétien governments. Likewise, Greek Canadians from Ontario, such as Liberal MP Jim Karygiannis and Conservative MP Gus Mitges, have successfully served in Ottawa.

Poles, along with Croats, claim to have participated in the earliest explorations in Canada. A Pole is said to have discovered Labrador in 1476. But significant emigration from Poland had begun only

He says intercultural competence is crucial when conducting business in a multicultural society. In the Arab world, Westerners soon realize they cannot do business with Arabs if they fail to recognize and respect their traditions. If a guest crossed his legs when seated in a way that pointed his shoes at the Arab host, chances are the million dollar business he was negotiating would go down the pipe.

In cultural learning styles, Jagelski makes some interesting observations. One is the fact that Asian cultures consider it impolite to reveal to another that what is said is not understood. "In interaction, therefore, a restraint of feelings and respect for authority do not permit many Asian individuals to make eye-contact, something that Westerners tend to misunderstand.

His notes on multicultural health are useful observations for people in the medical profession. In Arab countries, he says, patients are told only the good news about their condition. Among African communities, it is considered uncaring of the physician to tell the family that the individual who is terminally ill is going to die. Most South Asians are not accustomed to being informed about the negative side of their treatment. The Western model of informing patients can lead to confusion and fear, he says.

Jagelski's handbook also provides a set of skills applications to specific situations, sensitivity pointers and so on. He says that if we recognize the importance of intercultural competence for professionals, whether they be in health, education, justice or business, this work will, at least, point the way to how we can make multiculturalism work in Canada.

after its partition in 1795 spurred as well by political and religious oppression and a poor economy in those years.

The sons of Polish immigrant arrivals fought with distinction on the battlefield in the War of 1812 and the Rebellions of 1837. Later, prompted by the vigorous policies of Clifford Sifton, Minister of the Interior in Wilfrid Laurier's government, some 115,00 Polish settlers came to Canada between 1896 and l918 to settle the newly opened prairies.

Sir Casimir Gzowski, an exile of the 1830s who reached Ontario in the early 1840s, was knighted for services to his Queen both as a military and a civil engineer. Gzowski was responsible for seven bridges (including one connecting Fort Erie, Ontario, with Buffalo, New York), ports, canals, railways, Yonge Street between Toronto and Simcoe, the Niagara Parkway, and numerous other engineering projects.

Most of the

Cohen recalls discrimination against Jews

When Lee Cohen told students at the erstwhile Halifax West High School graduation ceremony last summer that their mission ought not to focus on becoming doctors, engineers and lawyers, but instead to "make a difference and change the world." one thought for a moment he had exploded some dynamite in young minds.

There were young people who came up to the podium and were decorated with medals and Governor General awards. But there were others who won nothing. Just as well, Cohen had struck a note of confidence when he said what he said, making them realize as did the blind poet Milton many years ago that : "They also serve who only stand and wait." Making a point about his own schooling that at first seemed purposeless, Cohen said it was that advice calling on him "to make a difference, that spurred him to take up law."

Lee Cohen

Cohen, whose law practice in Halifax is dedicated to immigration and human rights, *post-war migrants were political refugees from a Communist regime. While the Depression slowed the movement of Poles into Canada, during the Second World War almost 1,000 Polish engineers, technicians, and other skilled refugees came to Canada and contributed to the war effort. After the war, ex-soldiers, who had served with the Allies, entered Canada on the strength of one-year contracts to work on beet farms, in factories and hospitals, and as domestics and railway builders.*

The Poles have always organized their societies along cooperative lines. When the banks were reluctant to advance funds to immigrants with meagre jobs, parishes and secular bodies across Canada created credit unions.

The first, St. Stanislaus Credit Union, was organized in Toronto in 1945. The 1996 census counted 786,735 people of Polish origin in Canada

The Portuguese

says he is motivated by a strong belief that all people have the unconditional right to live their lives in freedom and safety and that Canada must honour its international commitments to provide a safe haven for those escaping persecution.

"Canada has more people in jails and more child poverty than any other industrialized nation in the world. There are problems and racism is one of them," he says.

Cohen's view of Canada may have been shaped by life and work experience. He says he grew up like many others, experiencing the insult of bigotry and religious intolerance. "Today that kind of bigotry is complex, but subtle. Those that cursed you to your face 25 years ago, may not do it likewise today. But you still see victims of bigotry, only you cannot identify the oppressor," he says.

In his address to students at Halifax West Cohen recalled an unpleasant incident in his boyhood, when a bunch of white kids cornered him in the vicinity of his home in New Brunswick and swore abuses at him because he was a Jew. Cohen says he never feared being beaten before, but although the incident frightened him, he took an escape route and ran across to the store next door for refuge. What followed left him cold again. The storekeeper was reaping absolute joy from the confrontation.

Cohen grew up witnessing the hostility towards Jews, fights between black and white kids, ghetto thinking – all of this at a time when Canada's immigration legislation was racist. "Legislation is a reflection of national thinking," he says. "I think Canadians are making a change. But as a rule, Canadians do not support immigration."

Much of Cohen's work takes place at the Immigration and Refugee Board (IRB), where he seeks to present a truthful case of persecution of any refugee whose trial in Canada sometimes appears to throw him between the devil and the *were among the other European settlers that travelled to Canada before the British and French laid claim to North America. The Portuguese records point to considerable activity in the North Atlantic in the Fifteenth century. The expedition of Diogo de Tervi in 1452 is said to have provided information for Christopher Columbus.*

According to another account, Joao Alvarez Fagundes, a Portuguese navigator, sailed along the south coast of Newfoundland and into the Gulf of Saint Lawrence and established a settlement in Cape Breton.

Portugal's role as an imperial power over the last several centuries resulted in Portuguese immigration around the world to its colonies from Brazil and Goa to Mozambique and Macao.

Over one million people left Portugal for Brazil between 1886 and 1950. But it was not until the Canadian and Portuguese governments signed

deep blue sea.

"I think there is unfairness in immigration at the basic level," he says. "IRB judges are political appointees, many who do not clearly perceive what persecution is in other parts of the world. The point Cohen makes is that IRB judges tend to apply the Canadian skill of judgement to determine the truth. That parameter of judgement, he says, which cannot conceive of the human capacity to endure torture and not report it, works detrimentally to any case.

"It takes a sophisticated thinker to realize that a refugee has had to lie in order to live," he says. "Religious, cultural and political repression in other parts of the world do not allow a victim to report, say, a rape incident. What Cohen is saying is that a refugee who has had to lie and mistrust people in order to flee cannot understand the dynamism and culture of this country. That must be taken into account.

It's ironic that Cohen has been able to establish trust with a clientele that is largely Arab and Palestinian. "Having to fight cases of refugees from Israel has forced me to look at the Arab-Israeli conflict from the other side. And because I deal with human issues, I have seen what the universality of mistreatment is all about."

Cohen may still be nursing those early wounds. But that was quite clearly a major step in his education. That was something that taught him to look at people, like people - where neither colour, nor religion nor race can colour one's judgement.

labour contract agreements to supply railway construction and agricultural workers after World War II that Canada became a popular option for Portuguese immigrants for the first three decades following the war. In the 1996 census it was estimated that as many as 335,110 people of Portuguese heritage lived in Canada.

Emigration out of Eastern Europe

Like the Poles, Croats also claim to have participated in early explorations. Two Croatian soldiers, Ivan Malogrudie from Senj and Marino Masalarda from Dubrovnik came to Canada with the expedition of Jacque Cartier in 1534 according to some accounts.

Croatian voyagers accompanied the fur trade and joined the Cariboo gold rush of the 1850s as well as the Yukon rush of 1898. A group of miners made their way from the United States to Vancouver Island and at about the same time, Croatians established settlements around the Fraser River salmon grounds and got integrated into the Canadian fishing industry.

The pre-war movement of Croatians to Canada resulted in settlements across

Hungarian refugee recounts his escape during the revolution

A reflection by Yolan (Erdos) Bensik

We huddled each night around our radios for the news from Budapest. I saw five pointed stars in our town square, weighing many tons, tumble to the ground. Political prisoners were freed from jails. As the army troops moved in, the fighting escalated. Each night we had our clothes by our bed ready to flee if they were to bomb our part of the town.

The borders opened in October 1956. My father wasted no time in planning our escape. He was tired of the constant pressure on him to join the Communist Party - not having any money for the necessities of life and often times taking only a slice of bread with lard as his lunch. Our landlord accused my father of threatening to shoot his dog, although we did not even own a gun. But the landlord was a communist party member and so the trials went on and on. That finally pushed my father to leave.

I did not understand what the whispering was about between my father and a young newly wed couple (Kocsis, Antal) that rented a cot in our kitchen. My sister Eva (Erdos) who was six years old and I, who was eight at the time, were told that we were going to visit our relatives, but this couple never came with us. None of our relatives knew about our plan to leave Hungary because my father thought that if they knew, they would somehow detain us.

As the hours passed we walked some miles, took a ride on a truck loaded with soldiers, then on a truck that carried pigs - the driver of which turned out to be the husband of a relative. My inner instincts told me as we hitch-hiked that this was definitely not the way to either of my *several regions of Canada including British Columbia, Alberta and Saskatchewan.*

They worked in mines, forests and factories. By 1910, Croatians were migrating to Winnipeg from the United States. But Croatian miners also sought opportunities in the new mines in both northern Ontario and Quebec. In the Atlantic provinces, by the mid-1920s, Croatians had settled in New Waterford, Reserve Mines, Stellarton, and Sydney in Nova Scotia.

The better educated immigrants came to Canada during the interwar period and looked for work in the industrial cities of central Canada. Most of the internally displaced persons (IDPs) from World War II refugee camps in Austria and Italy—these were Croatian educators and other professionals, skilled tradesmen and industrialists – were relocated to remote resource towns to work as bushworkers, miners, and railroad navvies.

grandparents' homes.

As we walked we got wearier and wearier. My dad had to carry my sister and me alternatively. From time to time we would ask dad about when we would be reaching our destination, or which was the home of the relative near the Austrian border or about who would guide us across it. He would point to a light in the distance and say: "That's where it is". But it always seemed like it was another light away. We were definitely not going to visit grandma, this I knew.

It was October 30, 1956. The escape itself was not unpleasant. I remember the green grass, it was a sunny day, it all seemed very easy. The Red Cross was there to aid us as we crossed the border to Austria. They helped to direct us to hostels. As a child of eight this was a strange and different place but to my dad this was freedom: to think, to plan for the future, to dream. He was 34, and my mother was 26.

We liked Neikirchen in Austria a lot with its mountains and pretty scenery. This is where I tasted my first orange. The scent was like a heavenly perfume. Oh, those Austrian chocolates! I can't forget the strange brown drink they called Coca Cola and which I first tasted in a café. My dad was offered a job if we stayed but he declined. His dream was to go to Canada and nothing would change that.

We lost the young couple when they were transferred to another location, never to hear from them again. The barracks were getting empty one by one as people were heading to different countries of the world. Then came our turn. We took the train from Austria to Genoa in Italy in December 1956 where we were to board the Venezuela, but not before locking my parents out of the hotel room when they went out to see the town. They had to break the door open even as we were sleeping so soundly.

Deep waters always scared me and this

time I was petrified when I first cast my eyes upon the *Venezuela*, the ship that was to take us to our new homeland. The trip across the Atlantic was 12 days long. The food was Italian and very strange because I had not eaten anything other than Hungarian food till then. There were about 1,500 refugees aboard - everyone eager to reach their individual places in the new country.

Our ship stopped in Morocco. The merchants sold their rugs and brass ornaments... this was a lovely city. I can still remember the warm weather in late December. That was the very first time I had seen an African man. They kept busy playing chess and cards and were very relaxed - definitely very different from East Europeans.

The Venezuela made its way across the Atlantic to Halifax. I remember as I was laid up in hospital on the ship, admitted for sea sickness along with my mother, a baby boy was born on board. I recently got in touch with his parents in Toronto.

The *Venezuela* made its way across the Atlantic to Halifax. I remember as I was laid up in hospital on the ship, admitted for sea sickness along with my mother, a baby boy was born on board. I recently got in touch with his parents in Toronto.

As the ship approached Canada the weather got colder and colder. After 12 days of just being sea sick, losing weight on my already frail frame, we pulled into Halifax, January 1957.

The army cadet band greeted us. We were then ushered into the immigration building to be

In striving to survive the oppression of invading powers, some four million Croatians have left their home over the years - many migrated to Canada - and estimates reveal that there are about 250,000 Canadians of Croatian descent.

The most significant periods of Croatian migration to Canada were immediately after the two world wars. Thus today there are Croatian communities in Toronto, Vancouver, Edmonton, Calgary, Winnipeg and Montreal.

In time literary and cultural societies, sporting clubs and musical groups mushroomed paving the way for Croatian culture to be handed down to their children. The first Croatian Catholic church was established in Windsor, Ontario, in 1950. Other parishes and missions were located in Toronto, Mississauga, Hamilton, Sault Ste. Marie, Winnipeg, Calgary, and Vancouver.

Croatians have

played an important role in many sectors of this country's development. Early Croatian migrant workers helped build the transcontinental railroad and develop Canada's mining, forestry, agriculture, and fishing industries. During the interwar period, many became diligent factory workers in Canada's growing industrial sector. The third generation has enjoyed considerable upward mobility, building careers in the service, industrial, private, and professional sectors of Canadian society.

Croatians have notably demonstrated great talent in the visual and performing arts.

Famous among them were Nenad Lhotka who headed the Royal Winnipeg Ballet during the 1950s and Joso Spralja who excelled as a painter, sculptor, photographer and folk musician during the 1960s. Likewise Croatians have been celebrities in sport—hockey, football and heavy weight boxing.

examined by doctors. We watched TV and ate corn flakes for the first time without milk as one would eat potato chips. My parents were very enthusiastic and full of life and had plans for the future.

We then boarded the train for Timmins Ontario, a mining town where we would spend the first six years of our lives in Canada before moving to Toronto, Ontario in 1963. It seemed like the train ride from Halifax to Timmins would never end. The Christmas decorations were still out on the houses which I found very pretty. The adjustment to Timmins was not easy.

I was the only one in a track suit. The kids in school thought I was wearing pajamas.

My father went to work in the Hollinger Gold Mines for a while until he was able to open his own tailoring shop. My mother was an excellent cook and just as well opened her own little restaurant. This was a social place for the young refugees who found work in the mines.

We moved to Toronto in 1963. My father later went on to manufacture ladies wear. My brother, who was born in Canada, became an aircraft technician. My sister worked as a Word Processing Operator at the Ministry of the Environment. I worked in a medical laboratory and later married a jeweler. We now run a jewelry manufacturing business in Toronto.

Life in Canada has been a rich and rewarding experience. I am definitely happy that my parents had the courage to dream and to make that bold decision, so long ago, to come to Canada.

Courtesy: Pier 21 Society

Among the best known Croatian Canadians are the Mahovlich brothers of hockey fame, George Chuvalo - the Canadian heavyweight boxing champion and figure skaters Sandra and Val Besic.

According to one account the first Czech to have come to Canada was Brother Peter Pandosy, a Bohemian Oblate who founded the mission in 1858. But significant Czech immigration to North America began only after 1860.

In 1918, at the end of the first World War, the Austro-Hungarian empire had fallen and Czechoslovakia was formed. Political descent over the Czech nation's destiny within the Austro-Hungarian empire as well as poverty had forced the movement of Czech immigrants to Canada.

Most of the early Czech immigrants to Canada settled on the prairies in southeastern Saskatchewan and in 1900, a few Czech

Kosovar doctor recalls the nightmare of war

When the war in Kosovo got ugly and Dr. Luli Rrafshi's wife was nine months pregnant, he had cut short his Residency at Bucharest to be with his wife at this critical time. Then seven days after the NATO strikes began, the Serb forces began a brutal expulsion of Albanians.

"Tanks were parked outside my house in Pristina," Dr.Rrafshi says. "The soldiers were burning houses, and shooting in the streets. NATO planes were bombing through the night. We escaped to a friend's house at safe distance from the tanks. But that was momentary comfort.

Rrafshi says that night the police officers nabbed them and ordered them out of their homes. "They yelled at us, kicked the others and asked for gold and cash."

Rraffshi

Luli Rraffshi and his wife

families who came via the United States founded Prague (Viching) in Alberta. The first urban settlements to receive pre-war Czech immigrants were Edmonton, Kingston, and Windsor, while Toronto drew only a small transient group of Czechs at this time.

The first Slovaks came in the early 1870s drawn by work opportunities in the coal mines and steel mills of the United States. But ten years later, many of these same immigrants moved into western Canada, drawn by the prospect of obtaining free homesteads while others hoped to earn a better living in the coal fields of Alberta.

In 1885 a group of Slovaks and Hungarians from Pennsylvania established settlements in the farming districts of Manitoba and Saskatchewan. But in time, many began the trek eastward to other small urban communities in northern Ontario.

Between the

tells an interesting tale here. He says he gave away the keys of his car and some cash. But they asked for more. So he proffered his wedding ring. The constable looked at it and said he wouldn't take that because wedding rings are sacred. Luli thought to himself: "Here's a criminal afraid of God."

Along with some 10,000 other Albanians Rrafshi and his wife were being expelled that night. He remembers the silent march to nowhere. Many thought they were being taken to the killing fields. He says Albanians were beaten with rifles on the way and were finally put on buses and trains and moved to the Macedonia border where many died.

Rrafshi was lucky. UN personnel fought their way with Macedonian officials at the border and got him and his wife into a camp and three nights later she delivered a baby girl at a hospital. He then went shopping for refugee status in the tents where American, Australian and Canadian immigration officials were interviewing refugees. He turned to the Canadians and the following morning saw his name on the list of those to fly to Canada.

The war may be over. But the scars remain. Last year he travelled to Kosovo with Canadian friends. "The people had changed. So many were still in a state of trauma, hopelessness, many without their homes, their relationships were cold. And there were minefields everywhere," he says.

Rrafshi believes it's going to be very hard for Serbs and Albanians to be friends again. War has taught everyone that it achieves nothing. It only destroys. The wounds will take a life time to heal. He remembers stories told to him in the camp: The story about the old man with four women and lots of kids who said he was living to protect his daughters in law – after his four sons were killed in his presence. He recalls the story about the family that *wars (1920 and 1940) Romanians, Slovaks, Czechs, Hungarians, Poles and Ukrainians were among those interned in camps in Western Canada. The political air in their European homelands had obviously contributed to some ideological polarization among European ethnic groups.*

The political ideology, however, that most worried the Canadian government was communism. It was strongest among Ukrainians and Jews who had been radicalized before the war.

Later, growing class consciousness of immigrant workers in the 1930s found expression in left wing activity - although those who participated in left-wing activism faced the threat of arrest and deportation.

While a small percentage of the Czechs who began coming to Canada at the time were farmers, the vast majority of postwar arrivals came to the cities, particularly to Montreal,

was leaving home in their tractor and was stopped by soldiers who dragged their daughters away and shot the son, leaving the father to bury him. Rrafshi's father who now lives with his daughter in London was almost killed during the war – beaten brutally with a knife at his throat.

Does he hate Serbs. No, he hates the criminal, because as they say, you do not condemn the sinner, you condemn the sin.

Today in Canada, Rrafshi works for a pharmacy biding his time as he re-qualifies in medicine. At the end of this year he finishes an examination that will see him begin Residency and work as a Clinical Associate.

The memories of Greenwood in Nova Scotia where he first arrived are still very fresh. "Canadian hospitality was overwhelming," he says.

Kosovar artist sees light at the end of the tunnel

Zeqirja Rexhepi's church murals in Kosovo tell stories of Christian history. Rexhepi is a Muslim, who explains his interest in Christian painting very simply: "Christians are my brothers. We were all Christians before the Turkish repression, anyway," he says pointing to one of his murals on film. It was clear that Rexhepi was saying even religion may be an accident of birth.

His paintings were destroyed during the Kosovo war, which erupted after Slobodan Milosevic, upon coming to power, sought to amalgamate Albanians in the autonomous province of Kosovo within the Serbian federation. People of Albanian origin, prior to *which quickly replaced Winnipeg as the largest Czech settlement area in Canada until World War II.*

In 1938 Nazi Germany invaded Czechoslovakia and annexed it. As a consequence many refugees fled to Canada. Among them was businessman Thomas J. Bata who relocated staff from the Bata shoe factories in Moravia to this country.

But Czechoslovakia had its share of troubles once again after 1957 when a Stalinization process had begun: the secret police infused terror, many Czechs were thrown into jail and collectivization of land got underway. On August 24, 1968 Czechoslovakia's democratic structure had been completely shattered by the Soviets and the Czechs remained suppressed under communist rule for another 20 years. In 1968 almost 12,000 Czechs emigrated.

The 1996 census figures, based on self-declared ethnic

Albania's independence had settled in Montenegro, Macedonia, Greece and Kosovo.

In the heat of the war, when NATO planes began the bombing in the rump Yugoslavia, Rexhepi had to flee with family. Most of his paintings in post-war times and since coming to Canada are thus about the ugliness of war, the joys of freedom and the comfort of peace. And in those paintings, sunrise is always a dominant factor. "We waited for sunrise to leave home for the Macedonia border," he says. "We waited for sunrise for the NATO bombing to begin. We waited for sunrise to leave the camp in Macedonia and fly to Canada."

Rexhepi spent a month in that camp with his wife and six children. He says there were at least 30,000 people in those tents and that living conditions were abominable. The children, at a point, were critically ill.

In taking the decision to leave that refugee camp, Rexhepi chose Canada. His wife wasn't sure about that at first. "Canada is very far away," she had said. But Rexhepi explained, pointing to Kosovo from the Macedonian border: "It's only 12 miles away. But for us it's a million miles today."

The Rexhepi family was first hosted at Greenwood in Nova Scotia. The welcome reception, he says, was overwhelming – especially for people who hadn't seen water for weeks.

But Rexhepi had left behind a whole lifetime in Kosovo. That included 25 years as a teacher of art, the many church murals, the performing arts theatres where he gave violin recitals, those festivals in Europe at which he made official representations.

"After a week of painful thinking, I realized I would have to begin from zero," he said. "But where could I begin?"

He began from the very beginning - with

Zegira Rexhepi: I must never forget where I have come from

origin rather than place of birth, recorded a total of 71,915 Czechs 45,230 Slovaks and even 39,185 persons who were content to be labeled Czechoslovakian.

The Czechs and Slovaks have formed several socio-cultural and political organizations in Canada, which have become nerve centers for calendar events of the Czechoslovakian community. Many Czechs have been attracted to business and industry, while larger groups have established factories of their own—the

children. When he saw children at the camp in Greenwood play with water colours, he went up to them and taught them a lesson in art. The following day Canadians at the camp wanted to identify the artist. "From there on, I saw the light at the end of the tunnel. The government gave me a grant. I was commissioned for exhibitions – Canadians invited us to their homes. I was even presented with a violin."

Rexhepi is an accomplished violinist and, in Canada, has performed for the Salt Water Moon and at several other concerts. His paintings have universal themes. The "Open Window" is a perspective on Canada's welcoming door in the midst of civil strife across other parts of the world. Another painting "Nostalgia" which portrays a solitary flute player is about the sentiment of home.

But why should he have any sentiment for home? Rexhepi says he can give to Canada nothing if he abandons his roots. "I want to contribute to Canada. But to do that I must never forget who I am and where I have come from."

biggest being the Bata family's shoemaking empire.

Like the Croatians, the Czechs too have been active in the visual and performing arts. The famous among them are conductor Walter Susskind, composer Oskar Morawetz, pianist Antonin Kubalek, and actor Jan Rubes and his actor wife, Susan Rubes.

Slovak immigrants too have played important roles in business and industry as well as in sport and politics. Stephen B. Roman achieved rapid success with Deni Mines—regarded as being the richest uranium mine in the world. Slovaks in the news world include George Gross, former sports editor, Toronto Sun, and Robert Reguly, former writer for The Toronto Star.

One of the first Hungarians to travel to North America, according to some accounts, was Stephen Parmenius, chief chronicler for Sir Humphrey Gilbert's expedition. He is reported to have come to Newfoundland in 1583. But Hungarians speculate that a member of Leif Ericcson's expedition to Vinland around 1000 AD may have been Hungarian.

Explorers apart, Hungarian immigration to Canada may have begun only by about the 1880s. One report notes that Pal Oscar Esterházy brought Hungarian immigrants from the coal-mining region of Pennsylvania in the United States to settle in Saskatchewan. They lived in tents until family houses were built. Esterházy's dream, the report says, was to establish a "New Hungary" on the Canadian prairies. The town of Esterhazy, today, bears his name.

Essentially, it was economic and political upheaval that forced a majority of Hungarians to immigrate to Canada. In fact, many of those came from regions surrounding Hungary after the First World War, including countries from Yugoslavia, Romania and Czechoslovakia. The majority were tradesmen, who found work in Ontario.

Although immigration to Canada dropped during World War II, it picked up again after 1947. During World War II, German troops had occupied Hungary - hundreds of Hungarians were deported to concentration camps. But when Hungary was liberated from Germany after the war by the Soviets, immigration levels rose again.

Nonetheless, the strongest exodus of refugees from Hungary began during and after the Hungarian revolution of 1956 when Hungarians opposed the Soviets. The Soviet army brutally suppressed the revolution and put 35,000 people on trial. As a result, some 200,000 fled and many came to Canada.

The post World War II Hungarian immigrants that came to Canada set up several organizations, including the World Federation of Hungarian Veterans (W.F.H.V.) and the Royal Hungarian Gendarmerie Veterans' Benevolent Association. The Széchenyi Society, a Calgary-based group, was created to establish Hungarian credit courses. The Hungarian Helicon Society was founded in 1952 to preserve, explain, and promote the thousand year old cultural and historical heritage of the Hungarian nation.

The Hungarian Revolution in October of 1956 provoked a strong response from Hungarian Canadians which resulted in the establishment of the Hungarian Canadian Relief Fund in Toronto and creation of a blood bank. The Legion for Freedom was formed in response to hundreds of pleas received by relief organizers for the formation of an international brigade to aid Hungary. When the Hungarian revolution was crushed forcing an exodus of refugees, Canadian immigration officials responded generously to applications from Hungarians. Those fleeing the Revolution represented the brightest and best of Hungary's urban population. In total, approximately 37,000 Hungarian refugees were admitted to Canada following the 1956 Revolution. Nearly 20,000 Hungarian refugees settled in Ontario. In 1966, the tenth anniversary of the Hungarian Revolution was commemorated by Hungarian communities across Canada and a monument was erected in Toronto. The Freedom Monument is in Wells Hill Park on the shores of Lake Ontario, renamed Budapest Park at the time of its dedication.

The Hungarian House of Toronto became the Hungarian Canadian Cultural Centre – the largest in the Hungarian diaspora. The Krónika (Chronicle), the official monthly of the centre, was a cultural news magazine distributed in some 30 countries worldwide, until 1993.

Almost five million Hungarians live outside Hungary today. Over 160,000 have made Canada their home. Well-known Canadians include John Polanyi, winner of the 1986 Nobel Prize in Chemistry, Peter Munk, head of the construction firm Trizec and Dora Pedery-Hunt, sculptor and recepient of the Order of Canada.

Among non-British settlers to arrive in Canada at the early part of the twentieth century were Macedonians—people from the Balkan mountains at the time part of the Turkish empire. The first Macedonians were driven by a search for opportunity and by the varying degrees of political repression and socio-economic misery. They are reported to have lived almost a completely isolated existence in neighborhoods around their church, stores, and boarding houses.

The mass departure of Macedonians from Aegean Macedonia continued in the aftermath of the Second World War and the Greek Civil War (1946-49). The 1950s witnessed the arrival of about 2,000 Macedonian refugee children to Canada. Significant exodus from Vardar Macedonia (now the Republic of Macedonia), or from towns and cities, began in the post-Depression years and gained momentum in the postwar period.

The Canadian census of 1996, records 30,915 Macedonians in Canada, the sum total of individuals making single or multiple group responses. According to local sources, there are about 125,000 Macedonians in the Greater Toronto Area and the outlying regions, creating the largest Macedonian settlement outside the Balkans.

The war in the Balkans

The war in the Balkans was fought along ethnic lines in the early nineties and was obviously triggered by Bosnia opting for independence from the former Yugoslavia. The 1990 elections in Bosnia resulted in a governing coalition of three ethnically-based parties generally corresponding to the three major ethnic groups. Muslims and Croats in the governing coalition favoured independence for Bosnia-Herzegovina, while most Bosnian Serbs did not.

In a referendum shortly thereafter, over 63 percent of Bosnians voting chose independence, meeting the criteria for recognition set forth by the U.S. and the EU several months earlier. In the spring of 1992, after its offensive in Croatia had ground to a stalemate, Serbia launched a war of aggression against Bosnia. The nationalist Bosnian Serb political party, proxies of Serbian President Slobodan Milosevic, had removed its members from the government.

In March, Serbian paramilitary forces, reinforced by the Serbian-dominated Yugoslav National Army, began a campaign of terror in eastern Bosnia. In that time more than 200,000 Bosnians were killed. Tens of thousands of Bosnian Muslim women, many of them only girls, were raped. More than two million Bosnians became refugees or were in internal exile. Canada, like the other refugee welcoming countries, opened its doors to war displaced people from the Balkan war.

But on the heels of the Bosnian war, hostilities surfaced in the province of Kosovo. Milosevic was determined to amalgamate the minority Albanian community within the Serb federation and sought to do this by amending Yugoslavia's constitution. The Albanians put up resistance to Serb aggression and when Kosovo became a battle ground, NATO intervened and a bombing campaign ultimately brought all sides to the conflict to discuss peace.

Emigration out of Latin America

Emigration out of Latin America

The political and economic decline in South America in the last four decades drove hundreds of thousands of Spanish-speaking Latin Americans to seek refuge in the United States and Canada.

It was a time of political upheaval in Paraguay and Bolivia, the heyday of the Cuban revolution in the Sixties, military dictatorship in Argentina and Peru, the overthrow of Chilean President Salvador Allende and civil war in Central America.

After the three hundred year domination by the Spanish monarchy, Latin America may have finally got its freedom at the turn of the nineteenth century. But political and social change, since, has been marked by military dictatorships and turbulent

Brazilian doctor says success has taught him humility

Dr. Tirone David says that leaving home in Brazil was no challenge and that even today while holidaying in his country, he has the urge to come back to Canada. "I do not know the precise reason for that. I am a workaholic and love what I do. My wife and eldest daughter are Americans, my other two daughters are Canadians. I enjoy our lifestyle, our (Canadian) customs and culture. Actually, I prefer our way over the Brazilian way," he says.

David says he was raised in a multicultural family and was taught to accept other cultures and customs. His father is from Syria and his mother from Italy. "The differences, however, are becoming less evident because we are all changing towards a global commonality," he says.

David left Brazil to further his education. "I was very inquisitive during medical school and believed that Americans were at the cutting edge of medical frontiers. I wanted to be part of that and acquire the "know how" and ultimately return to Brazil someday." He graduated from medical school and chose to do his surgical training in the United States. He began as an intern at the State University of New York in Brooklyn in 1970 and from there went to Cleveland Clinic and finally to the University of Toronto.

He says that by the time he finished his training at the University of Toronto in 1978, he was already "over-qualified" to practice in Brazil and no university in Brazil had the infrastructure he needed to continue his academic career.

"Doctor Wilfred Bigelow, then Chief of Cardivoascular Surgery at Toronto General Hospital, made me an offer I could not refuse," *times – although there have been fleeting experiments by democratic republics towards self government - the type one sees in Costa Rica.*

Uruguay lost its grip on free government after dictatorship got a foothold in 1973. At about the same time, Chile replaced its democratically elected president with a military dictator. But although dictatorships got deeply entrenched in the body politic in Bolivia, Cuba, El Salvador, Honduras, Nicaragua and Panama, there is evidence of political growth there.

Peru and Columbia had made some progress toward constitutionalizing democracy, but corruption and social ills have almost knocked it apart. Alberta Fujimori (the Japanese-Peruvian) set up a corrupt government taking the economy to chaos and in Columbia the reign of terror unleashed by drug lords on the streets of Bogota have cracked the fragile

he says. "I stayed and I am glad I did. Today I have Dr. Bigelow's job."

Dr. Tirone David

David has developed several operative procedures to treat patients with complex cardiac diseases over the years. He has presented his research and clinical findings at national and international conferences. His academic focus is centred on heart valve disease, complications of myocardial infarction and aneurysms of the ascending aorta and aortic root. "Most of my contributions have been in this area," he says. "For instance, the perfect artificial heart valve is yet to be developed and for this reason we try to repair rather than replace heart valves. This is David's special field of expertise.

But he is also the inventor of the Toronto SPV, a porcine valve manufactured by St. Jude Medical from St. Paul, MN. "We are now experimenting with a newer version of this valve: The Toronto Root and the Toronto SPV-II.

Success has taught David the virtues of humility. "My father had a major influence on my character," he says. When I was young he was demanding and always expected more than I could deliver. He has mellowed with age. But now at 94 he is still my hero. When I finished medical school he gave me a gift and card that *democratic structure. In Panama, the country's first woman president Mireya Moscoso who oversaw the transfer of the Panama Canal from the United States has vowed to "bring a true democracy to Panama."*

The Chileans saw turbulent times in the 70s and 80s when, a Marxist government took the reins of power led by Salvador Allende. The confiscation of property and the economic chaos that followed, led to swift emigration out of Chile. Then later in 1973, a group of generals led by Augusto Pinochet overthrew Allende and seized power. The subsequent years until 1990 were marked by a reign of terror, arrests, disappearances and repression of political dissidents.

Canada did not turn a blind eye to the human rights abuses that forced thousands of Chileans to flee the country. While some migrated to other Latin American countries including Cuba, some

read: "May it never develop in your mind that you know everything and your education is completed. You will always be a student." He was absolutely right. I remain a student. I continue to learn and I have an incredible appetite.

What does David think about the future of Canadians. "I think Canada is a wonderful country. I do have some concerns about our future but then again, which good citizen of any country doesn't worry about the directions the country is taking? I don't know if I can effect change the way any one single person wants. Commonality is inevitable. I believe people get the government they deserve. Canadians are changing and they dictate our future. This is a complex issue because it involves economics, politics, religions, cultures and all the other variables that affect society."

His sense of humility is reflected in what he says in the end. "I think it's patronizing to go on and on with my opinions. They are unimportant because they reflect only my own."

Bolivian neurologist furthers the threshold of restorative neural surgery

Twenty years ago when he came to Canada leaving his home in Bolivia, he went to community college to study English. Today, Dr. Ivar Mendez is in Halifax to push forward the threshold of neural transplantation.

Neural transplantation is about restorative brain surgery where cells are taken from the skin and implanted on the brain. It is, for the first time, going to achieve new gains in the treatment of Parkinson disease and spinal chord injury.

A modest man with great humility, Mendez left Bolivia in the early eighties when,

Dr. Ivar Mendez

after a military coup, the country swept through bad political times and universities were closed for a couple of years. Mendez's father, a physician at the time, teaching at La Paz university decided to move the family to Canada.

In April 1981, Mendez came to Ottawa interrupting his freshman studies in the seven-year medicine program in Bolivia. But he more than made up for any losses. Within a year of his

others migrated to Soviet bloc countries and yet some others to Canada. Ottawa had by then implemented a special immigration program for Chilean refugees. In total, about 7,000 Chileans are reported to have made their way into Canada.

Indeed, in some other Latin American countries – Gautemala for example, Canadians walked the extra mile to set up solidarity networks and lobby their governments on justice issues.

The political instability and terrorist group activity in Argentina in the Seventies brought waves of Argentinians to Canada swelling their immigration numbers to about a thousand every year. The 1996 census put the count of people claiming Argentine ancestry to 7,115. While the greatest concentration of Argentinians is in Ontario and Quebec, there are also smaller communities in Vancouver, Calgary and Edmonton. Although those that came in the early seventies took up jobs as electricians, mechanics and construction workers, the Argentine community in Ottawa, Montreal or Vancouver today is composed of professionals – university professors, scholars, physicians, architects, engineers – as well as entrepreneurs.

Perhaps the most famous Argentinian in Canada is Sergio Marchi who came to this country as a young boy in 1959. Almost 25 years later he was elected to parliament and was appointed cabinet minister in Jean Chretien's government in 1993. In his last ministerial portfolio Marchi served as Canada's foreign minister and is currently the country's Ambassador to the World Trade Organization.

Since the Nineties, Canada's relations with Latin America has assumed another dimension as a result of trade groupings. In 1989, it became a full member of the Organization of

arrival in Canada, Mendez graduated with a B.Sc at the University of Toronto and was accepted into the medical college at the University of Western Ontario. Graduating in 1986, he entered a residency training program for neurosurgery, during which time he completed a Ph.D. in transplantation –Anatomy and Neuro-biology. "I remember I was among the few at the time pursuing transplantation," Mendez says.

When he won the William P. Van Wagenen prize for Neurosurgery Residents, he finally possessed the resources to pursue his interests in Sweden where he went to work with the father of neural transplantation, Anders Bjorkland.

Two year's ago Mendez was recipient of the Royal College Medal Award for Surgery which recognizes his outstanding contribution, particularly in the field of neural transplantation for Parkinson's disease.

"Repairing the brain will be very important in the future," says Mendez, who is the Head of the Division of Neurosurgery at QEII. "Initial results are extremely promising. Mendez has, in fact, invented a surgical instrument to plant cells into the brain. The hospital holds the patent.

His Ph.D. in anatomy gives him a double-edge for he is also a famous sculptor. Mendez says surgery and sculpting are complimentary. "Sculpting helps me look at disease from a holistic viewpoint." He is currently sculpting the bust of his former professor, Dr. Charles Drake, who became famous worldwide for developing techniques for the repair of the ruptured brain.

Although Canada is home to Mendez today, he travels to Bolivia twice a year to carry out operations in small communities and contribute to societies that have nothing. "It's no big deal. It's a drop in the bucket for

American States (OAS) – an intergovernmental organization formed to promote economic cooperation.

In 1994 it signed the North American Free Trade Agreement (NAFTA) which opened trade doors to Mexico. Two years later it signed a similar agreement with Chile investing billions of dollars in that country. In 1998, it hosted a regional conference on international migration issues.

Although Mexico's political culture was not visited by military dictatorships, one party rule by the Institutional Revolutionary Party dominated its history for clearly seventy years. That party stronghold was finally broken last year when Vincente Fox breezed into power.

Just as well, Mexicans made tracks to Canada in a significant way only in the Seventies. That was a time when professional cadres and students seeking admission to Canadian universities were emigrating out of

Bolivia who needs so much more. But that little is something I need to do," he says.

Bolivia is, obviously, close to his heart. "In essence all of us are the same," he says. "Bolivia is poor and life is a struggle every day. That is why I appreciate opportunities in Canada. I think my Canadian identity is enriched by my Bolivian heritage, just as my Bolivian heritage is complemented by my Canadian experience."

In much the same way, says Mendez, Canadians should appreciate the fact that immigration is a two-way street. "While Canada provides the opportunity as a host country, immigrants provide the skills. That must not be overlooked."

"It's like success. It's not accomplished alone."

Trinidadian lecturer says nationhood and race determine who you are

The mind of the newcomer to Canada has a vantage point. The cross-cultural experience and the experience of the developing world's brush with the factors of confrontation, inter-religious conflict, the racial divide, repressive governments and the vicious cycle of poverty build new thinking thresholds for people from developing worlds that Canadians are probably never going to experience.

Isaac Saney, born in Dublin, educated in Trindad and now a lecturer at Dalhousie and Acadia universities speaks almost passionately about these things. Saney's mother is a Black Nova Scotian, who married Isaac's father – a Trindadian with ancestral roots in India – when he was studying in Canada.

Mexico city, Puebla, Guadalajara, San Luis Potosi, and Acapulco in search of better economic opportunities. According to the 1996 census, there were at that time 23,295 people of Mexican descent in Canada.

Mexicans can be found across the spectrum of economic life in Canada as professionals, entrepreneurs, manufacturers, or construction and agricultural workers. But while they have keenly sought to integrate with mainstream Canadian society, Mexicans hold fast to their heritage. The proliferation of Mexican restaurants truly reflects that observation.

In the second half of the last century, Canada has pursued economic cooperation with Brazil as well and joint ventures have since been established. But because Brazilians cherish family ties, emigration out of Brazil was limited until the crises of the Eighties.

Middle class Brazilians then turned to Canada for a better

It's just as well that Saney has some strong feelings about other worlds – the racial divide and nationhood. Although he could have chosen from among three citizenship opportunities, he says he feels very Trinidadian. "I like to think or feel like an international citizen, but I feel Trinidadian."

Saney teaches Black world history and the international development studies program at

Isaac Saney

Dalhousie University and was, sometime ago, working on several papers on Cuba.

Making a point about pride of race and nationhood, he says the Blacks in Cuba see themselves as Cubans first and foremost unlike the Blacks elsewhere where the pride stems from being Black first.

On nationhood, he says: "Isolationism is about staying away from the bad world. But the environmentalist notion that the world can be destroyed by one environmental factor reminds you of the oneness of humanity."

Having said that, he thinks both nationhood and race are one of the very vital factors in determining who you are. "I don't think people are inherently racist. The whole concept of race makes no biological sense. It's a *life and most of them settled in Ontario, where the significant Portuguese community became catalysts in their integration, providing linguistic familiarity and jobs for the once colonized Portuguese-speaking Brazilian immigrants.*

Today the Brazilian Carnival Ball is a prestige event on the social calendar in Toronto and Brazilian music is promoted through the many mushrooming bands.

Latin Americans have brought to the Maritimes of Canada, what is truly music to the ears. Latino Nites are a regular on the social calendars of downtown clubs.

Likewise, Latin Americans have brought with them the sport closest to their heart. Jose Farias Martinez, the international soccer referee in Canada is reported to have said: "The only language we did not have to learn on coming to Canada was the language of football."

socio-historical construction originating from the myopic view of history."

He makes an interesting observation about the transition from acceptance of cultural diversity to the shift to a racial divide, which he says evolved at the beginning of the Columbus era which ushered in slavery and later colonization.

"Prior to that, there was a notion of the acceptance of peoples based on culture, not race. The effect of that shift can be seen even today in the vast disparities: the civilization of the West versus the economic underdevelopment of Africa, debt in the Third World and the siphoning off of interest payments into the West, unequal trade and so on. In saying so, he makes the point that the "inferior" versus the "supremacist" phenomenon is probably a product of economics.

Saney came to Canada for his tertiary education after completing high school in Trinidad. He graduated in Political Science, did a Masters in International Development Studies and has just completed a law degree at Dalhousie University. He currently holds a permanent faculty position at Dal as well as teaches at other universities including Acadia and Saint Mary's Universities.

As a lecturer on Cuban development affairs, Saney naturally holds some strong feelings about Cuba – and especially about what he calls the unjustifiable criticism of Cuba's socialism. "Cuba's international brotherhood has never been appreciated although it was the only country that shed blood fighting South African troops outside its shores," he says.

He makes a positive point about the fact that Cuba's social justice must be seen from the facts: He says poverty is confined to less than 10 per cent of the population and that 85 per cent of Cubans own their homes.

Cuban flees repression, comes to Canada as stowaway

Some doors just never open. "When Cuba shut the doors on us because of our political opinions, Canada opened its heart, but not its doors to opportunity," says Dania Soto.

Dania's husband Andres Diaz jumped ship three years ago and arrived in Halifax to claim refugee status. Andres was a hydraulics technician and worked for some years at the port in Cuba. "But I had to flee," he says. " I resisted forced involvement in the communist program and I was victimized."

Andres says job recruitment in Cuba is linked to compliance with Fidel Castro's communist program and that any dissidence is not tolerated. So when Andres chose not to go with the political tide, he found that he would have to flee.

"Six days in the hold of the ship were a nightmare," he says. "The weather was freezing and I remember having to share my food and even clothes with fellow stowaways." In Halifax, Andres got a hearing at the Refugee tribunal and was granted refugee status. So what is he complaining about?

In the first three years since arrival in Canada, Andres had worked in a bakery, on a ship, in a recycling plant and was laid off work in a construction company. So he delivered pizza for a bit. "What else could I do? I studied hydraulics engineering at a community college in Cuba but that's a qualification

"Six days in the hold of the ship were a nightmare. The weather was freezing and I remember having to share my food and even clothes with fellow stowaways." In Halifax, Andres got a hearing at the Refugee Tribunal and was granted refugee status.

Canada does not recognize. I cannot afford to re-qualify because if I do not work, who will feed the family? What future can you see for myself?" he asks.

Dania was an accountant in Cuba. But in the nine months since her arrival in Halifax, she was turned away by employers. "Accounting is accounting in any language," Dania observes. "If there are accounting systems that I am not familiar with, I can be trained. But why turn me down? I strongly feel Canadian employers tend to ignore immigrants," she says.

So in a sense, Andres and Dania felt like they had been thrown between the devil and the deep sea in their early years in Canada. They have had to give up Cuba for what they believed was wrong. But having said that, they have shut those doors permanently. "The Cuban consulate in Ottawa may never issue us a visa for home. That means I may never see my mother again," Andres says.

Having fled Cuba, Andres believes he must be discreet. "Walls have ears. There are Cuban security agents in all parts of the world, so I don't feel free to talk about Cuba," he says. "My family in Cuba may be harassed if I do." But he says he chose to flee Cuba, because he could not submit to Castro's communism, and where, he says, 80 per cent of the people are double-faced.

Canada may have its heart in the right place. But jobs stand in the way of settlement of newcomers. Indeed, social assistance and unemployment insurance are systems in place. But not everybody is comfortable with charity.

"They say: no Canadian experience, no jobs," says Dania. "But the reverse is true as well: No job, no Canadian experience."

It's just as well that foreign credentials recognition is now beginning to become an issue that' s getting a hearing. A major conference in Toronto held sometime ago helped to put the spotlight on the need to establish equivalency of credentials especially with countries from where today's immigrants originate, so that doctors, engineers, accountants or lawyers who have come to Canada on the basis of the assessment of their professions may be absorbed into the job market.

In other provinces of Canada, focus groups are studying problems connected with the access to professions and trades and are investigating the entry process for several professions, including teaching, engineering and nursing. The focus groups say they are working towards recognition of competence-based assessment alongside credential-based assessment.

Mexican gives Canadians a mouthful

Mexican-born Ana Jenkins is going places, quite literally. The restaurant Mexico Lindo, which she opened two years ago on Convoy Street in Halifax has moved. What does that mean? "That means more traffic, perhaps a licensed bar and some live entertainment," she says.

Jenkins came to Canada not for the usual reasons: political instability, state repression, poverty, children's education, taste of freedom, or the lure of a better life. She

Anna (centre) and William Jenkins (right)

came here to live with the man whom she first knew as a pen pal. Wilson, her Canadian husband, tmanages the restaurant while she gives the food a touch of Mexico.

Jenkins is a busy bee when at work, has a ready smile and a sense of excitement in her communication. It's thus surprising she should say that the first few months in Canada depressed her enormously. "Canada was another planet altogether. I grew up in a small community in Mexico. The people were open, warm, willing to talk to anybody," she says. "But in Canada, I realized people kept a distance. It's also a different business culture which makes doing business a difficult thing for people like us."

Jenkins says her husband told her not to expect Canadians to be warm as they are in Mexico. "Canadians don't mean exactly what they say….or at least that's how my wife feels," he says.

Mexico Lindo - the restaurant, was her first brush with business. The decision to open a truly Mexican restaurant was automatic. "Halifax does not have authentic Latin food. The other Mexican restaurants are run California style," she says.

Mexican food is unto its own with its blend of spices just as its rice servings with tomato, corn and garlic and several peppers is uniquely Mexican. The restaurant's Tamales must be tried. This is a kind of donair of corn flour dough filled with chicken and topped with salsa. Vegetarian chilli does not appeal to Jenkins. "I try to give people what I got at home. And vegetarian chilli did not originate in Mexico," she says.

Fresh tortillas made of real corn, chilli made Latin style (more beans than beef) and Mexican desserts are a staple on her menu. Jenkins uses spices brought from Mexico, which makes her food a delicacy not for the faint of heart or palette. The prices, especially on the beef burrito, are like music to the ears. The new Mexico Lindo outlet is soon going to include a Mexican spice store and a tortilla factory or bakery.

The Jenkins couple took the Immigrant Entrepreneur Program at MISA (Metropolitan Immigrant Settlement Association) before venturing into business. But, of course, like other immigrant entrepreneurs, Jenkins has had her share of troubles.

"The government funding agencies do not believe in small projects or in retail business. Banks told me I didn't have a credit record. But how can I, when I've just set foot in Canada," she asks. Calmeadow finally forked out a small loan.

But Jenkins knows today that it takes time and a lot of hard work to succeed. In her business, she says, she's got to be able to turn people away from the Tim Hortons' habit in order to sample the spice of another world.

Her customers are a mix of US tourists and local residents. Jenkins proudly points to her guest book on which names such as Alexa McDonough figure. "But of course, McDonough didn't want us to do her anything special," she says. "She said she was an ordinary person."

Now she believes she's uncovered the three secrets to success: location, location, location.

Young West Indian wants a career in social justice

War and poverty had forced Cherise Adjodha's grandfather out of his home on the Turkish-Syrian border about the time when a

Cherise Adjodha

hostile anti-Christian environment had sent many Christian Lebanese fleeing to other parts of the world. He settled down in the Caribbean and raised his daughter there, who later met with Indian-born Girvan Adjodha and married him.

"It wasn't a good mix in the cultural pot," Cherise says looking back at her youth. "I never felt accepted in dad's family and somehow grew up feeling contempt for the sense of morality among some of their men folk. Mom and dad have, anyway, gone separate ways."

Cherise is a charming, young girl, who on some days screeches out the Judo cry, her hands drawn forth for a martial attack, while at work. On other days, Cherise talks about Einstein's relativity and humanity, laments the fact that people in the Vatican wear rich robes, that the story of Adam and Eve should have been told the way it is - and thinks that sin and guilt are a product of man's misguided notion of what is wrong.

Cherise went to school in the Caribbean, although she was born in Canada. She came back to Halifax after graduating from high school and did a double major in Sociology and Philosophy. She was, early this year, a volunteer coordinator at Oxfam and was doing an internship with the Youth Mine Action Ambassador Program (YMAAP) in Canada.

Returning from an orientation trip to Cambodia, last year, Cherise says, people there would rather take the chance venturing into mine infested fields to get food than go without it. She says there are about four to six million mines in Cambodia – a result of the 1973 US bombing of its borders. "There are cases of people dying from tampering with bombs in their backyards. There is thus a whole generation of people who are amputees," she says.

As an intern with YMAAP, Cherise had made several trips to schools to heighten awareness of the landmine problem and other development issues including the current Oxfam campaign against Sweatshops. As many know, Sweatshops employ primarily women and children at below minimum wages, exploit them, and in some countries, beat and chain them and even force abortions if their women employees get pregnant. She says many conglomerates are involved in this – contracting their work to Sweatshops in Third World countries and turning a blind eye to the abuses and exploitation people suffer.

According to an Oxfam finding, only 0.4 per cent of a $100 pair of a top brand of shoes goes out in wages.

What are Cherise's goals? She thinks she will have achieved something when the work she has initiated can sustain itself. She is hoping to see a catalyst that will link Canada and the Third World and address problems that deal with the exploitation of people.

"People won't rise above poverty, if they are constantly under stress," she observes.

Lebanese-Trinidadian plunges into politics

When election fever grips Canada, the media buzz in NDP leader, Alexa McDonough's campaign office, is stirred by a relative newcomer to Canada. Anthony Salloum, who is McDonough's media coordinator in Ottawa is usually piecing together news bits and speaking up passionately for the party's manifesto these last couple of years.

Salloum was born in Trinidad of Lebanese parents. His father had moved to the Caribbean in the early half of the century, about the time when the Turks were retreating from Lebanon and an anti-Christian backlash had forced Christian Lebanese to flee to other parts of the world including Brazil, Venezuela and, of course, the Caribbean, through trade vessels.

"There was always that dream to return home," says Salloum. So sometime in 1971 the family made tracks to Lebanon. As most would probably know, that was bad timing. In 1975, civil war broke out in Lebanon unleashing violence on the streets and forcing the Salloums to leave once again. Canada opened its doors.

Salloum went to school in Canada and for a couple of years found that his English language skills were challenged making interaction with peers difficult.

Those language skills were no longer challenged by the time Salloum fell in love. It wasn't puppy love. "Politics has always been my first love," he says. "But at the time, there were many Lebanese

Anthony Salloum (right) with NDP leader Alexa McDonough and Lebanese Prime Minister

who plunged into politics out of a sense of gratitude to Pierre Trudeau who had opened the flood gates of immigration during the civil war.

Trudeau's ideas about Canada had initially drawn Salloum to the Liberal party. But by 1996, he says, he felt abandoned by the party with its slant towards right wing social and economic policy – when it failed to do away with the free trade agreement as promised, to abolish GST as promised and pushed for the drug patent act which has taken up drug prices for ever.

Salloum says he's a social democrat at heart and had joined the Liberals when, at the time, the party was preaching a social policy.

Where does Salloum think he would be in ten years? "I don't know," he says. "If Alexa McDonough decides to leave politics, I'm out of a job. But I will likely continue in the field. I am an activist and want to work in advocacy or anywhere I can effect social change."

Salloum says he works with a politician who can influence change and that allows him to participate in the process. "I think our immigration policy is misguided. It's not family centered, but focused on economic benefit. The policy is less humane. Consequently, the word "immigrant" has become a negative connotation.

Salloum says we need to shake up things a little. McDonough urges immigrant communities to get involved in the system. "Tell people what your challenges are. Do not think there is no room for you in the political process," she has said.

"Ours is an intimidating society," he says. " I believe we can be more sensitised about the needs and challenges of new Canadians. We have the capacity to do so."

Salloum says one has seen a greater influx of Gulf Arab Muslims into Canada these last few years. "I've been sensitive to the negative reaction to their presence here." He refers to the sense of curiosity with which mainstream Canadians look at the Muslim lady's *hijab* or head cover and assume that it has to do with spousal repression.

El Salvador lawyer flees, advocates for refugees

Francisco Rico-Martinez finds the big question "What if?" haunting him all the time. "If I go back to El Salvador, I could be President? If I go back , I could be killed?" It's a refugee syndrome, he says.

Rico-Martinez was a lawyer and economist in El Salvador, at the time, investigating human rights abuses by the government. He obviously was doing a good job because in a flash he was reported missing. The military regime had seized him and threw him into jail and no one knew about his whereabouts for a week.

El Salvador was in the midst of a civil war at the time and intellectuals were increasingly targeted. But pressure from the Jesuit Refugee Service, finally got Rico-Martinez released. He had to, nonetheless, flee for safety.

At the time Canada had set up a special refugee program for El Salvadorians and Rico-Martinez was recommended to the Canadian Embassy. By a special Minister's Permit, he got his landing papers and came to Canada after a brief transit in Gautemala.

Despite his training as a lawyer and economist, Rico-Martinez could not obtain credentials recognition, but because of his law and Human Rights background he plunged into work connected with refugee settlement. He and Loly, his wife, joined FCJ Hamilton House – an organization, in Toronto, that provides shelter to single women and legal aid and support to refugees.

In May 1990, The Sisters, Faithful Companions of Jesus (FCJs), a Roman Catholic religious community, entered into a joint Project with the Jesuit Centre for Social Faith and Justice to operate Hamilton House as a shelter for refugees. Any rental income from the Project was to be used by the Jesuit Centre for other projects benefiting refugees. Francisco and Loly Rico were among the first to live in this house. They had intimate knowledge of the situation of refugees, having themselves had to flee from El Salvador and come to Canada.

In June 1991, Francisco and Loly Rico expressed interest in operating the house as a shelter for female refugee claimants and their children who were living in abusive situations.

Francisco Rico-Martinez with lawyer Richard Soo

When the Jesuit Centre withdrew from the original agreement, the FCJ community entered into a partnership with the Rico family to take over the operation of the house and the FCJ Hamilton House Refugee Project was born. The Ricos shared the house with women in need and their children.

When the policy change in Legal-Aid created a void of free, legal assistance offered to refugee claimants and cutbacks in social assistance in Ontario made it impossible for refugee claimants to hire private lawyers to defend their case before the Immigration and Refugee Board, FCJ Hamilton House applied to the Maytree Foundation for a grant to develop a new program of public education.

The program was intended to offer free training workshops in basic immigration law and in the process of refugee determination, to people in community agencies that dealt with refugee claimants. The Maytree Foundation offered a grant to support this new program and the ***Refugee Help in Refugee Hands Project*** began in April 1997 and Francisco Rico-Martinez began to work full-time on the project.

"....Canada is still not fully meeting its commitments to the UN Conventions and Universal Declaration."

But Rico Martinez is also President of CCR (Canadian Council for Refugees) an advocacy organization and government watchdog that reviews policy and legislation connected with immigrants and refugees and finds solutions, makes recommendations or lobbies against policies it thinks do not serve the cause of refugees.

How does Rico-Martinez feel about nationhood. "I have never asked that question to myself," he says. He says pensively: "Perhaps I belong to El Salvador as much as I belong to Canada. I feel sorry about what my country did to me. But the only way to act is to work toward stopping torture and dedicating my life to settling the refugees of the world. I have the skills for that."

He says he recalls mental images of El Salvador with some nostalgia. "They cut me off. They destroyed my future. So I live today with the big question haunting me. There are so many possibilities, should I decide to go back. One is that I could be killed. That's a refugee syndrome," he says.

Looking at the opportunities in Canada, Rico-Martinez says that although Canada does better than the other refugee accepting countries, it is still not fully meeting its commitments to the UN Conventions and Universal Declaration.

The Exclusive/Inclusive clause that does not give a person charged with a criminal record in his country a chance to file before a refugee tribunal in Canada is against the Convention, he says. The other two refer to the detainment of minors in Canada and refugees left in limbo in Canada.

Emigration out of the Middle East

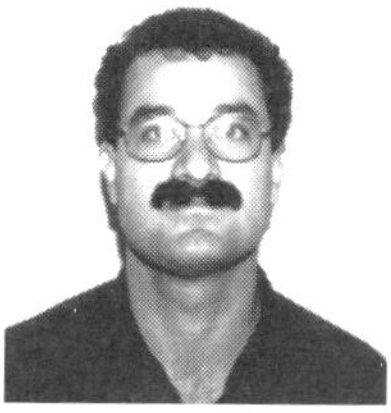

Emigration from the Middle East

Most of the Lebanese who came to Canada are from one of the many religious and cultural groups which lived in harmony until 1840. But that tranquil state had ended in 1841 after a dispute between a Druae and Christian family in Southern Lebanon when both enlisted their co-religionists and a year of military skirmishes began. Just as well, between 1860 and 1880, a new chapter in the travels of these latter day Phoenicians had opened. Foremost among the political and economic developments that forced Lebanese Christians to leave the motherland was the severity of anti-Christian violence by Druze militants and their Turkish Moslem allies.

According to one author, the first

Iraqi journalist flees Iraq after enraging Saddam Hussein

When in the wee hours of January 16, 1991, the United States and its allies began the bombing of Baghdad in Iraq, the world woke up to the reality of a war being fought by one man against the might of 27 nations of the world. That man was Saddam Hussein, the protagonist in the Gulf War, who ten years later is still standing his ground against UN sanctions and the oil export embargo.

Sabah Al Lami, at the time, editor-in-chief of *Al Mustaqba* (The Future) had been hobnobbing with the Iraqi leader in the post-Gulf war years, counted among the elite in the media, a front-row journalist at news conferences in the Presidential Palace. In those years, Lami was cautiously speaking out against injustices and human rights abuses witnessed in Iraq. "I did this discreetly, never confronting the President directly, but pointing some

Lami (right) with Iraqi President Saddam Hussein

modern Lebanese to arrive in Canada was a Mr. Nader from Zahleh who settled in Montreal in 1883. The first Lebanese arrived in Nova Scotia in about 1885 via New York and eventually settled in the Sydney area of Cape Breton island. The two decades which followed constituted the formative period in the settlement of the Lebanese in Canada.

But since Lebanese were considered Asians by Canadian immigration authorities, Lebanese and Syrian people wanting to immigrate were prevented from doing so. Just as well, widespread protests broke out among communities and according to one report, the term "Lebanese" fell into some disfavour because of its rhyme with "Japanese" and Chinese".

In May, this year, the Lebanese plaque at Pier 21 in Halifax was unveiled as a tribute to the many Lebanese that touched shore at Pier 21 ever since 1884.

questions in his direction," he says. But apparently Lami was walking a tight rope and in early 1998 played into Hussein's hands with an editorial titled: Freedom of Hell. The Iraqi leader was outraged and ordered his imprisonment for six months, along with other eminent journalists in Baghdad at the time. Lami says he was sent to Al Radhwaniah jail and the experience was like being thrown among lions, where prisoner beatings were commonplace.

The jail term served as reflection time for Lami, whose book "*Maqalad azajad Saddam Hussein*" took shape then. The title translated in English reads: "The stories that enraged Saddam Hussein".

When he had done his six-month term at Al Radhwaniah, Lami was put under house arrest and the President's office ordered his name to be blacklisted at Iraq's border exits. But he was determined to flee the repression. "There's nothing money cannot buy in Iraq today," he says. Lami says he bribed a Passport department official about US$1,000, who discreetly erased his name on the blacklist, issued him a new Passport in the name given at birth, by which he was not known, and on November 6, 1998, he crossed Iraq's border into Jordan.

In the following months, Lami hired lawyers to change family records, declare his wife dead and register a new name. Once again he forked out some US$5,000 to a Passport department official to ease the way out of Iraq for his wife and six sons. He says, his other colleagues under house arrest who preferred not to pay their way out of Iraq were rearrested at the border points from where they attempted to flee and were thrown again into jails.

Lami and his family spent the next two years in Jordan where he wrote prolifically for the London-based Arab magazine *Al Zaman* and published his book *"Maqalad azajad Saddam Hussein"*. At the same time, Lami also

But perhaps the biggest influx of Lebanese immigrants into Canada was witnessed closer to our time, when Lebanon's civil war broke out in 1975.

The war goes back to the 1940s when exiled Palestinians welcomed into Lebanon, strengthened their militant base there, prompting an aggressive response from Israel. Consequently, Syrian troops moved in making it a hotbed of violence, pitting Muslims against Christians in what came to be called Lebanon's 15-year "civil war."

The Lebanese in Canada, like the former day Phoenicians, have been successful merchants, many of them are in property development, construction, hospitality and, of course many are professionals."

But outside the Levant, significant Arab emigration into Canada began only after World War II. President Abdul Nasser's government and his revolution of 1952 which introduced

applied to the United Nations High Commission for Refugees (UNHCR), seeking refugee status. Two years later, he was welcomed by the Canadian government.

His book "*Maqalad azajad Saddam Hussein*" comprises a series of articles on the human rights abuses and injustices witnessed in Iraq frequently. One of them is a story of the displacement of some 500 Shia families who had moved to Baghdad from Southern Iraq just prior to the Gulf War.

"Hussein's government organized the complete demolition of these 500 houses by tractors," Lami says. "The civil conflict that erupted after the Gulf War was a reflection of how much Hussein felt threatened by the Shias of Iraq – an Islamic sect opposed to the ruling Sunni government.

Lami, who was present at most of Hussein's Press briefings at the Palace prior to the bombing of Baghdad, says the Iraqi leader was absolutely aware that the war would devastate Iraq, but decided to take his country to that brink.

"The oil embargo on Iraq is not an evil act of the United Nations or of the United States," he says. "Hussein is the real killer of those children dying without food or medicine. In order to perpetuate his regime he ordered his commanders to sign agreements on all UN conditions of surrender."

Today, freedom is Iraq's No. 1 priority, Lami says. Canada has taught me a lot about what freedom is and what it is to "think free". On the other hand, there are perspectives to freedom, he says. "I had the freedom to smoke wherever in Iraq. I don't here," he says with tongue in cheek.

communist social policy may have hastened the exodus of young Arab Islamists out of Egypt in the Sixties. The Fulbright Grants at the time beckoned young Arabs to the United States – many of whom began studies at Indiana University. In tandem Islamic organizations mushroomed and those included the Muslim Students Association and the Islamic Society of North America. In time, organizations evolved out of professional bodies and some of them today include the Association of Muslim Scientists and Engineers, the Islamic Medical Association and other advocacy groups lobbying against the discrimination of Muslims.

Arabs in Canada do believe that they are challenged by the media stereotypes. War in the region and terrorist attacks that have originated in the Middle East have somehow given Arabs and Muslims a bad name in the West.

The negativism, many Muslims believe,

Kurdish farmer escapes Iraq's chemical poisoning

It would seem natural to expect that settling down in another country, hit by the culture shock of white faces and foreign custom, would be a cakewalk for anyone who has eluded the watchful eye of a secret service agency or fled in the face of a chemical poison attack. But that's not always true. That's the painful dilemma of transition for some newcomers to Canada.

Haaji, a Kurdish farmer from Shimaal in the north of Iraq woke up terrorized one morning having learnt that some 5,000 people in the neighbouring villages of Halabjah were killed in a chemical poison attack ordered by Iraqi President Saddam Hussein in 1988. That day Haaji saw some 40,000 Kurds, like a sea of humanity, making a silent exodus out of Iraq and a forced entry into Turkey. "It was impossible to stay back. Saddam's army was shooting men and taking their wives and children away to be left at camps," he says. "I ordered my mother, wife and nine children to rise and leave."

In the dead of night, Haaji got his mother and three children to mount a pony, while he led the rest of the family on the two-day long trek on foot to the borders of Turkey.

The active Kurdish resistance in Iraq had begun in the early eighties which ultimately forced Saddam's army to get brutal. The Kurds who have been fighting for a homeland – despite recognition by the UN as a sovereign nation - have been scattered across Southern Turkey, Northern Iraq, Syria and Iran. There are about four million of them.

Haaji's exodus was like an unending saga of trials and tribulation. His daughter was lost in the melee one night, forcing him to make *has resulted in discrimination against them. The September 11, terror attacks on the US has intensified that negativism.*

In the last two decades, the Middle East has been torched by violence and repression of its people. The repression of Kurds in southern Turkey and Northern Iraq, the Lebanese civil war that started in 1975, the Iranian revolution and the overthrow of Shah Mohamed Reza Pahlavi, the persecution of the Bahai's in Iran, the Palestinian uprising, the Iran-Iraq war and finally the Gulf war after Iraq invaded Kuwait in 1990 were major contributors to the exodus of Arab families.

The Iran-Iraq War (1980-88) was spurred by religious schisms, border disputes, and political differences. Iraq launched the war to consolidate its rising power in the Arab world and replace Iran as the dominant Persian Gulf state. Iraq and Iran had engaged in border clashes for

a sinuous retreat. On his way back, he lost his mother, but reunited again at the Turkish border. They continued the trek only through the night and hid in the caves of surrounding hills in the day to avoid being seen by Iraqi soldiers. His cousin's wife, on the journey, who was about to deliver a baby, was confronted with the fact that her 18-month child in arms was about to die. "One moment she was burying a child, another moment she was giving birth to one," he says. But fleeing has it quota of troubles and Haaji's were not any different.

Upon approaching Turkey's border, Haaji got to know that Turkish soldiers were actually handing over Kurdish refugees back to Iraqi forces. But he took heart and with help from United Nations peacekeepers he was brought under UN protection and accommodated in a refugee camp on Turkey's border.

Haaji lived in those refugee camps for four years. "It was like hell. People were dying for the lack of food and blankets. Turkish soldiers were poisoning the bread that was being distributed to Kurdish refugees. There was no work," he says. Haaji and his family lived in those refugee camps for about four years before consular staff from Germany, the United States and Canada got there and extricated refugees from their plight granting them refugee status under the Convention Refugee Act.

By 1992, Haaji and his family were welcomed into Canada along with 300 other Kurdish families. Ever since, he has received social assistance from the Canadian government. But he is not a happy man. "Unfortunately, my children do not know about my culture," he says regretfully. "We are surrounded by Christians – not that there is anything wrong with them, they are nice people. But I want an Islamic environment for my children," he says. He thinks Canada is a good country and that Canadians are friendly people. "But our culture *many years and had revived the dormant Shatt al Arab waterway dispute in 1979. The Iraqis also perceived revolutionary Iran's Islamic agenda as threatening pan-Arabism.*

Ayatollah Khomeini, bitter over his expulsion from Iraq in 1977 after fifteen years in An Najaf, vowed to avenge Shia victims of Baathist repression.

The Iran-Iraq war lasted nearly eight years, from September of 1980 until August of 1988. It ended when Iran accepted United Nations Security Council Resolution 598, leading to a August 20, 1988 cease-fire.

Casualty figures are not accurate, though estimates suggest there were more than one and a half million war and war-related casualties - perhaps as many as a million people died, many more were wounded, and millions were made refugees.

Currently, there are three million Iranian refugees awaiting

is different. My children do not anymore go to public schools because I do not want to lose them." Unfortunately, he believes he has lost one.

Haaji's eldest daughter has left home. "She abandoned our sense of discipline and walked out," he says with much sadness in his voice. His wife explains: "She's under the care of Children's Aid and we are not allowed to see her. This in itself is hell. Nobody is even trying to bring us together."

He admits again that he likes Canada but does not approve of its laws, apparently decrying the system that believes the state must intervene in parent-child disciplinary affairs. Now because he wants his children to have an Islamic environment, he volunteers at a Muslim school in Canada in order to pay for his children's tuition fees. He says he cannot work for health reasons.

Haaji has the creature comforts that Canadians desire to be happy. But he is not. There is a sense that you can flee from hell on the ground, but you cannot easily flee from hell in the mind.

Egyptian film-maker is helping Arabs identify their roots

Tareq Abu Amin left Egypt in 1994 to study in Milwaukee before he moved to Canada. He realized almost immediately that he was in the midst of a personal crisis. "I suddenly became aware that I was different, not because of my colour - language was never a barrier - but because of my thinking mode, my value systems *decisions by authorities in Turkey.*

Likewise, there are as many Kurdish refugees. In 1998 when the Iraqi President Saddam Hussein ordered a chemical attack on villagers of Halabjah, some 40,000 Kurds, like a sea of humanity, made a silent exodus out of Iraq and a forced entry into Turkey. The Kurds who have been fighting for a homeland – despite recognition by the UN as a sovereign nation - have been scattered across Southern Turkey, Northern Iraq, Syria and Iran – and there are about four million of them.

The sweet smell of freedom in Canada must have been irresistible to the people of Iran in the after math of the Islamic Revolution of 1978-1979 which toppled the government of Shah Mohammed Reza Pahlavi. Initially the trickle was from military personnel and supporters of the old regime. The Iran-Iraq War and both religious

were different," he says. "What I thought was cool, was not cool to my peers. Thus feeling accepted became a major crisis of sorts."

A young man at the time, Tareq grappled with the problem, trying to understand his roots and the significance of roots in his life. "I had to identify what made me different and soon I realized that music best manifested that difference. The contrast of cultures had to be expressed. I had to share it with someone who did not share my roots. Music provided that contrast."

Radio Egypt – the weekly programme on

(L to R) Hakim, Mohammed and Tareq

Dalhousie University's CKDU in Halifax was a product of that crisis. Tareq launched Radio Egypt with the 30 cassettes he had left home. He says that in the first few weeks of hosting the program, he had played back some music and told a few jokes and invited the community to participate.

But in time, Radio Egypt created ripples. Tareq says other Arab communities felt under-represented and consequently "Arab Voice" was launched in 1996.

and political repression subsequently provided the impetus for the middle class and the Bahai's, the largest religious minority in Iran, to follow in their footsteps.

The imposition of the hijab (veiling) as mandatory female attire and the general marginalization of women forced those who did not share these values to leave Iran and many chose Canada.

According to the 1996 census, there are 64,405 Iranians in Canada, many of whom live primarily in Canada's largest cities.

The earliest immigrants from Iran quickly joined the professional ranks as medical doctors, engineers, lawyers, nurses, and dentists. Those who came later chose to set up businesses, focusing on the creation of construction companies, restaurants, bakeries, dry-cleaning shops, grocery stores, repair shops, and computer stores.

He realized the need to broaden the scope of the program to include realms other than music to open up an understanding of Arab culture.

At about the same time, he met with Mohammed Sabe, Saif and Hakim and together the group expanded the scope bringing political and social issues and current affairs in the Middle East into the program.

The Arabs, justifiably perhaps, feel they inherit a stereotype in the West that is unfair to them. Conflict in the Middle East and the slant with which it's reported in some sections in the media have given the Arab a bad name in the West. The Western world has been accused of thinking of Islam as militant by the natural extension of the stereotype of the Arab as terrorist.

Radio Egypt today is hoping to bridge those gaps in understanding. A year ago, Tareq and his colleagues on the team launched the program "Through Arab Eyes" which hosted scholars in Canada in talk shows to debate the Palestinian issue, the stereotyping of Islam, the sanctions on Iraq and so on.

Mohammed Sabe, who is graduating in political science at Dalhousie says the program has hosted scholars such as Dr. Tom Falkner for a perspective on comparitive religions; Dr. Barbara Petzen of Dal's history department on sanctions against Iraq and Dr. Mark Ellis of Bangor University on Peace in the Holy Land.

CKDU has recently been granted approval to upgrade its frequency range and it will thus be possible for more avid radio listeners to tune in.

But although Tareq believes *Radio Egypt* can be likened to a journey in which he has discovered himself, he must become aware of the fact that he is, in fact, the brainchild of something bigger. The program is catalytic in many ways. It is, firstly, helping other Arabs to discover themselves, identify their roots and stay in touch with home. On another threshold, the program has a job of educating non-Arab listeners on the cultural patina of the Arab world in order to bridge understanding on political and social issues in the Middle East.

Tareq, who is now an independent film maker as well as Mohammed Sabe have career callings to address. But as they groom a set of younger men to take on the mantle of hosting the program, they should not lose sight of the bigger picture.

Lebanese regrets father's assassination

Daniel Bertolmaos was only two years old when his father was shot in the head. Lebanon was in the midst of a civil war at the time. Bertalmaos alleges it that it was the politicians in the drug trade who organized the killing to eliminate his father, then a detective in the Lebanese government.

Daniel Bertalmaos

The hostile environment and fear that the children might also be targets of violence forced the family to emigrate to Canada in 1978.

Bertolmaos says he was growing up at a time when young men in Lebanon were charged with a sense of nationalism and the notion of dying for a cause was the spirit of the day.

He went to school in Canada, but his mother was never too happy to see him estranged from Lebanon. He says she wanted him to grow up with the noble ideals of his father, and so by 1985 when the war was simmering down, the family returned to Lebanon.

A chemical engineer, who recently graduated from Dal Tech, Bertalmaos is torn by love and loyalty to roots and home. "I cannot deny my roots," he says. "But I am loyal to Canada. I am not bitter about Lebanon, but about its body politic. I am Canadian, but I am Lebanese first."

He says he has learnt to appreciate life. "When I see people who have experienced war but want to go back and build their country, I see a strong will there and the lesson that you must never give up."

They say man is a product of his environment and Bertolmaos is one of them. Upon returning to Lebanon, he grew up rebelling against the barricades of Syrian troops everywhere and a corrupt body politic in which people in power rose and fell.

The West, he says, was made to believe that Lebanon's civil war was about a Muslim-Christian conflict. "It was not that, at all. Politically and economically the war is still going on. The man who organized my father's killing is currently a member of parliament."

The West, he says, was made to believe that Lebanon's civil war was about a Muslim-Christian conflict. "It was not that, at all. Politically and economically the war is still going on."

He says this war goes back to the 1940s when the exiled Palestinians were welcomed into Lebanon. "The Palestinian movement began inside Lebanon and that brought the Israeli bombs down on us and consequently Syrian troops moved in forever," he observes. "This was not a Christian-Muslim war. If not for that war, I would never be in Canada."

Bertolmaos believes that in spite of the hostile environment, he grew up learning to cherish his father's noble ideals: of fighting for an independent, free Lebanon and even dying for it. But life in Lebanon hasn't changed much after the war, he says.

So, once again he made tracks to Canada in 1995. "The desire to feel free brought me back to Canada and I think moving back to Lebanon will no more be very easy for me." Bertalmaos is now contemplating leaving his second home for south of the border. "I am loyal to Canada, but I have to move on." He is obviously looking for greener pasture and he knows it's always greener on the other side.

Kurdish engineer leaves Syria in silence

Dilbur Khalil's grandfather was a Kurdish revolutionary leader who invested family wealth in the campaign for freedom in 1925, until Turkish forces assassinated him and others in the family, forcing his son Shaikhmius, Dilbur's father, to witness the bloody shooting.

Dilbur says her father was never able to live down the memory of that assassination. He resolved to lead the campaign where his father left it. But in a swift move by the Turkish government, Kurdish families were separated and Shaikhmius was sent to Syria.

By 1948, as Dilbur recalls, the first Kurdish republic – the Republic of Mahabad was established on the Iranian side of Kurdistan. So it was sometime later that Shaikhmius helped to form the first Kurdish party in Syria. It may well be worthy to digress a bit here.

The Kurds have been fighting for an independent homeland for about 4,000 years. There are about 35 million Kurds spread out in Iran, Syria, Turkey and Iraq and, of course, some are in other parts of the world including Scandinavia, Azerbaijan and Israel, where there are at least 200,000 Kurds.

The Kurds, who are of Aryan descent, originally emigrated from the Caucasus mountains. Thus even today the Kurdish language retains 80 per cent of the original Indo-European tongue

Dilbur grew up in Syria with "strong Kurdish education" and later married into what she calls a "filthy rich" family. Her husband's father, a leader of the tribe, owned acres of land and millions of dollars. But in 1994 Dilbur's husband had to undergo a liver transplant. He travelled to England, where the treatment failed, and he died.

The Kurds have been fighting for an independent homeland for about 4,000 years. There are about 35 million Kurds spread out in Iran, Syria, Turkey and Iraq and, of course, some are in other parts of the world including Scandinavia, Azerbaijan and Israel.

The transition to Canada probably began at that point. Dilbur says the laws in Syria prescribe that should a wife lose her husband in death, she may keep the children only until they are eight years of age. After that she must transfer them into the legal custody of her husband's family. She says she did not appeal, because her husband's family was too rich and powerful to challenge in a court of law.

At the time, Dilbur worked as a design engineer with the Syrian government. That closed the doors to any travel outside Syria. Just as well, in secret, she applied to the Canadian embassy for immigration in the professional, independent category. Shortly afterwards, her credentials were approved by the Canadian Council of Professional Engineers (CCPE).

As if by coincidence, the Syrian government at the time asked Dilbur to attend an Engineers Workshop in Germany. That opened the floodgates to freedom. She flew with her children to Frankfurt, her Canadian Visa tucked safely in her son's travelling bag. Ten days later, in 1996, she flew into Toronto.

She brushes aside questions about loneliness and culture shock as factors that are not really challenging. The challenge, she says, was getting accepted as an engineer. "I applied, as required, to the Association of Professional Engineers of Nova Scotia. The test was very basic." But while she began the requalifying process, she says, she also did some technical support work for a small engineering firm.

"That was a nightmare," Dilbur says. "People told me they were using me. My peers told me I do not belong here. They admitted to prejudice among our managers." Then at long last came a job posting from Eastlink - a telecommunications company. She says she landed the job in three weeks, despite the fact that she did not hold a P. Eng. in Canada at the time.

Dilbur says it's a great company to work for. "I have never experienced discrimination ever," She started work as a systems design engineer approving designs for Cable TV networks as well as setting specifications and standards. But she's been pushed up the ranks lately and is currently the company's Network Design Manager. "Eastlink believes there may be just three people in Canada with my background in design," she says with some pride.

Iranian businessman brings health to food

Bassir Sobhani, whose Super Natural Food store chain in Halifax is winning new customers had seen it coming long ago. He left Iran in the mid-Seventies and travelled to Sri Lanka. Sobhani, at the time, had worked for Iran's largest gas appliance manufacturing company.

But leaving one's roots is not fun. He had travelled to Sri Lanka alone, leaving family and assets behind in Iran. Then in 1979 the Iranian revolution broke out. So while in Sri Lanka, Sobhani got married, had a son and started a modest grocery business.

Unfortunately, it was bad timing, he says. The Tamil insurgency tore through the tranquil environs of the sun-kissed island. "My brothers and I twice had hairline brushes with death, being caught in the crossfire of arson and looting. It was time to leave again."

Bassir Sobhani

It was just as well that the United Nations office in Sri Lanka opened his windows on the world and the Canadian government welcomed him home.

Sobhani has brought to Halifax, the Eastern affinity to natural foods. At the three Super Natural Foods stores, one sees a new breed of health-food shoppers buying preservative-free, non-toxic and vegan-dedicated foods and health supplements. Today he is taking new and mainstream Canadians along the naturopath with seminars and workshops that Supernatural Foods hosts for people willing to subscribe to this health mindset.

Of course, Sobhani too had teething problems settling down. He worked his way through a couple of jobs and did not get paid. "But hard work pays in the end. I finally bought the store, I worked for, paying up the money in three years," he says.

Sobhani's start-up problems also had to do with coping with culture shock. "Nova Scotians are a friendly people," he says. "I think I may have felt somewhat discriminated once or twice. But in those early days in Canada, I often laughed at a snipe, because I did not quite comprehend what was said. I am happy it was that way."

The Gulf War

August 2, 1990 -the day Iraq invaded Kuwait -was only a curtain raiser to the Gulf war. Behind the scenes, expansionist designs were already falling in place as Iraq was mounting a lame excuse for aggression, first condemning Kuwait and the United Arab Emirates for producing more oil than permitted by their OPEC (Organization of Petroleum Exporting Countries) quotas.

The UAE and Kuwait had already begun to implement cuts in oil output ahead of the OPEC meeting in Geneva then, when Iraqi President Saddam Hussein accused Kuwait of violating the Kuwait-Iraq border and stealing $2.4 billion worth of oil from Iraqi oil fields.

In a letter to the Arab League in Tunis, Kuwait refuted Iraq's accusations that it had erected military posts and drilled oil wells in Iraqi territory but also said that for several years it had quietly protested to Iraq about the occupation of part of its land by Iraqi forces. The two countries had fought a border war in 1973 but Iraq was a feeble military power then.

By July 15, mass Iraqi troop movements toward Kuwait's border, sent tremors through the world's financial markets as President Hosni Mubarak of Egypt launched a whistle-stop peace mission to avert a desert war between Iraq and Kuwait. The United States, which had seven warships on exercise in the Gulf expressed concern as 30,000 Iraqi troops moved towards the border after a week-long dispute over oil production and territorial claims.

A Jeddah mediation meeting between Iraq and Kuwait was finally arranged by President Mubarak and King Fahd bin Abdul Aziz of Saudi Arabia. The talks began on July 31, 1990, but collapsed soon after and Iraq massed 100,000 troops at the border and invaded Kuwait on August 2, 1990.

Iraqi troops supported by hundreds of tanks moved into Kuwait and seized control of the Emir's palace, radio and television stations and the airport in quick succession. The Emir, however, had left the palace before the Iraqis reached there and had flown to Saudi Arabia.

The UN Security Council condemned the Iraqi occupation (14-0) and demanded Baghdad's immediate withdrawal. Hours after the invasion, Washington ordered the aircraft carrier Independence and five escort ships in the Indian Ocean to head for the Gulf.

At the United Nations, the Security Council imposed the toughest economic sanctions in history on Iraq and Kuwait ordering an arms embargo and a ban on their oil exports. It also adopted 12 resolutions between August 2 and November 29, 1990 when it endorsed the use of force against Iraq unless it withdrew from Kuwait by January 15, 1991. But Iraq rejected the UN ultimatum.

On August 15, the Iraqi President told Iran he would withdraw from occupied Iranian territory and formally settle the 1980-88 Gulf war. Hussein believed the initiative would free his entire million-strong army for any conflict with the US-led forces.

In the meantime, several Kuwaiti citizens had fled the country and many sought temporary residence in other Arabian Gulf states.

On January 16, the US-led allied forces launched Operation Desert Storm in the dead of night with a massive air and missile offensive against Iraqi positions. By February 25, allied forces thrust into Kuwait and southern Iraq capturing 20,000 Iraqis. The following day, Iraq, its forces virtually surrounded, announced its withdrawal from Kuwait.

Iranian-born doctor explores minimal access surgery

Three years ahead of Ayatollah Khomeini's arrival in Tehran to establish the Islamic government, the Anvaris sent their teenage son for medical studies to England.

Dr. Mehran Anvari

Then later, when the family moved to Canada just prior to the Islamic revolution, the young medical student immigrated with his parents and younger brother to Canada but moved back to England to complete his studies.

Dr. Mehran Anvari is, today, the founding director of the Canadian Centre for Minimal Access Surgery at McMaster University, Hamilton, Ontario.

On completing his medical studies in England Anvari came to Canada and did surgical training at McMaster University. Later he went to Australia where he obtained his Ph.D. in gastrointestinal surgery.

But Anvari is steering research in a new field today: Minimal Access Surgery. The new science reduces pain and shortens the patient's length of stay at the hospital, enabling them to return back to work sooner. Anvari says there is now much expertise in this field and that minimal access surgery could soon be applied to all surgical problems.

Countries are going to go through these multicultural phases and Canada shall be regarded as a model state.

In 1999, he was instrumental in forging a partnership between St. Joseph's Hospital, industry partners and McMaster University to create the Canadian Centre for Minimal Access Surgery, where today research in the field is pursued, new procedures are evaluated and doctors are trained, while surgeons from across the world are consulted by the institution via satellite.

"Like never before," he says, "we are sharing information worldwide at the Centre for Minimal Access Surgery." Anvari says this field will progress a great deal more with applications moving to cardiac surgery, orthopaedics, urology, paediatrics and so on. "One will see the increased use of robotics to help surgeons to minimize mishaps," he says.

Turning to his life in Canada he says that while he may be proud of his own heritage, he admires Canadian society. "I believe in what Canada stands for and am proud to be Canadian." Making a reference to the fact that there is lesser integration of races in other societies such as Europe, USA or Australia, Anvari says he believes Canada is a template for future societies, "Countries are going to go through these multicultural phases and Canada shall be regarded as a model state. I have never felt like a foreigner in this country, because this is a tolerant society," he observes.

Iranian engineer invests in photo-finishing for a living

Small business is a big deal for Canada's economy. The 2.5 million small businesses in Canada account for 50 per cent of private sector employment and half of the country's economic output.

But newcomer Abbas Nadjafian says business in Canada is about "big fish gobbling up small fish". A year ago he opened Econocolour – a photo-finishing unit, but a couple of months later a superstore located in the same mall, opened a similar studio and has since threatened his livelihood.

"It's not competition, because a superstore does not rely on photo-finishing profits. It's only a service for its customers. But by its sheer size, it's forcing me out of business," he says.

He may be right. Immigrant entrepreneurs say the business culture in the smaller provinces of Canada is not suited for retail or international trade.

The banks tell you they are open to new ideas, but in reality it's another story. Everyone asks for proven Canadian experience and that's a Catch 22, they say.

But the more worrying factor, Nadjafian says, is that the "big boys" can juggle prices because of their financial strengths which allow volume shipment of imports to be made possible. That leaves no room for the small business entrepreneur to manoeuvre and consequently he is forced out of business.

Nadjafian's woes are echoed by other immigrant businessmen who say that there ought to be government support for small business even if it is by way of licensing and legislation. "There ought to be industry associations to lobby against monopolistic positions. "The big boys tend to lower prices until we go out of business and then they raise it again," he says.

But, of course, he is neither a photographer nor a businessman by training. A mechanical engineer from Iran, he was, prior to coming to Canada, awarded 30 major projects by the government of Iran, to build 18 gas and six oil pipeline networks.

Nadjafian had completed a tenth of the gas distribution network in Iran when he decided to uproot himself and the family and come to Canada. Once here, he says he could have made a definite contribution to the building of gas distribution networks in the province, but APENS (Association of Professional Engineers of Nova Scotia) threw in the road blocks. "Although my university in Iran was recognized by APENS, I was, regardless, required to re-qualify. I chose not to," he says.

Instead he invested $70,000 in Econocolour and hired one Canadian thus meeting the requirements set out for immigrant entrepreneurs.

Nadjafian is now looking to new opportunities. In Iran, he has helped in the transition from oil furnace systems to gas fired systems. He says he can see an opportunity of collaborating with companies in the future when the shift from electric stoves to gas stoves takes place. There's room for consultancy business there, when the need to supply pipeline installations in homes and offices becomes a trend, he says.

In Iran, he has helped in the transition from oil furnace systems to gas fired systems. He says he can see an opportunity of collaborating with companies in the future when the shift from electric stoves to gas stoves takes place.

Life in Canada, anyway, is not only about good or bad business, Nadjafian observes. "I came here for my children. They're okay. I'm okay."

Muslim scholar says Arabs are unfairly stereotyped

Stereotypes are, at best, stereotypes. Arabs and Muslims in the United States and Canada suffer them. Conflict in the Middle East and the way it's reported in some sections of the media have given the Arab a bad name in the West.

The Western world has been criticized for thinking of Islam as militant by the natural extension of the stereotype of the Arab as terrorist. "All these are misnomers and it's this negativism that discriminates against the Muslim nation," Dr. Jamal Badawi, says. Dr. Badawi, a Professor of Management at Saint Mary's University is also the Imam of the Muslim community in Halifax.

Dr. Badawi left Egypt when President Abdul Nasser's revolution of 1952 rolled out a new sense of communism and with it ushered in fear and oppression which ultimately hastened the exodus of young Arab Islamists in the Sixties. The Fulbright Grants at the time were, anyway, beckoning young Arabs to the United States – many of whom began studies at Indiana University. When he had completed a doctorate in management and a brief teaching tenure at the University of Maine, Dr. Badawi came to Halifax to take up a lectureship assignment at Saint Mary's University.

Jamal Badawi

Arab immigration into Nova Scotia began after World War II. Dr. Badawi says the influx began with a wave of Lebanese immigrants who settled in Pictou, Antigonish, New Glasgow and the Bridgewater areas. In the Sixties, the province had less than 200 Arab families but with their arrival, the evolution of Islamic organizations took root, starting out, as Dr. Badawi remembers, with the

Muslim Students Association and leading up to the formation of the Islamic Society of North America - a continental organization. In time, organizations evolved out of professional bodies and some of them today include the Association of Muslim Scientists and Engineers, the Islamic Medical Association and other advocacy groups lobbying against the discrimination of Muslims.

Dr. Badawi, a Muslim scholar, explains Islamic thought as well as spurs the formation of Islamic focus groups. He is a founding member of the Maritime Muslim Academy, a school for Muslim children in Halifax whose mission is to introduce Islamic values into the education process.

He says an understanding of cultures can change preconceived notions, remove bias and promote harmony.

"What's so old-fashioned about being modestly dressed," he says. "When you see a nun modestly dressed in white and her head covered, you turn to her with respect and appreciate the dignity of her habit. But when you see a Muslim woman with the *hijab* (head cover) you wonder if she is being repressed by her husband."

Murad Farid's boyhood years in Alexandria, Egypt

Family leaves Egypt with eighty dollars

Although Mourad's father was educated as a lawyer at the University of Sorbonne in Paris, he began life in Canada selling aluminium windows, door-to-door in Montreal. "I was a young boy of fourteen at the time and I don't think I fully grasped what the sacrifice had meant for our parents then," says Mourad Farid.

The Farids took the decision to migrate in 1962 when, during Gamal Abdul Nasser's regime, Egypt was transiting through social change . Most major private enterprises were being nationalized and communism was taking root. Farid's father saw a dismal future for his children in Egypt then. The family sailed on the *SS Cafe* to England and later on the *Empress of Britain* to Montreal arriving in Canada on October 10, 1962.

Having left behind assets in Egypt, the family had very little by way of resources which added to the problems of adjusting to a new society and culture. "My father had barely $80 when he landed," Farid remembers. "Getting a job today is a hill to climb. In the Sixties it was a bigger hill to climb for newcomers." Nonetheless, a few years down the road, his father went on to become a property manager and eventually a successful real estate broker.

Mourad says that his mother, who owned one of the most profitable boutiques in Egypt, took up a job as a clerk at Hemsley's in Montreal. She travelled to New York to stake her jewellery. She invested the money in a small antique shop which she called *Aladdin's Antiques*. In due course and long before it became the trend, she became an adult educator and taught Canadian history and antique refinishing. She eventually became a biological illustrator at the University of Montreal.

Farid also remembers hardship. "I remember that for the first two months in Canada we did not have a fridge, so we kept the food out on the balcony until the squirrels got it and we complained to the landlord. Eventually he got us a fridge. I remember that when we first arrived we did not have beds to sleep on and we had to bundle coats and other clothes on the floor to get some sleep."

But Farid is proud to be Canadian. He believes the future looks bright and he feels encouraged by the fact that in this wonderful country "we have the opportunity to talk about things, express our concerns and gain strength from our differences."

He tries not to dwell too much on some experiences of discrimination. He had studied at a Catholic school and went to Loyola University. When he was ready to embark on a career, Farid chose to teach. He applied to a college in Quebec but admission was declined - because of his religion. "The institution mailed me a letter to say that I could not be granted a teacher's certificate because of my religion." Canada was, apparently, a different country at the time and attitudes and systems were only then beginning to change and become less discriminatory.

Farid ultimately got to the top rungs in the insurance industry and especially at Manufacturer's Life. But now he says he wants to give back to the country that has given him so much. He serves on the board of a few immigrant service provider organizations, was executive director of MISA (Metropolitan Immigrant Settlement Association), founded the Action Group for New Canadians - an organization that advocated on behalf of newcomers and was, for sometime, Chair of ICANS - the Intercultural Connections Association of Nova Scotia.

PIER 21

Pier 21: The gateway to Canada in the twentieth century

Through the greater part of the twentieth century, immigration to Canada was essentially through two ports - one at Quebec and the other at Halifax. When on March 28, 1928 the Holland-American steamship *Nieuw Amsterdam* docked at Pier 21, Canada had opened its heart and its doors wider. In the forty or more years since its opening, the Pier welcomed more than a million Europeans, many of them refugees and war brides that endured World War II. The unassuming shed on the Halifax waterfront also saw the departure of 494,000 Canadian servicemen and women on their way to fight in Europe during the Second World War. As J P LeBlanc, the founding President of Pier 21 Society observed lately: "Pier 21 opened its doors to Kings, Queens, princes and paupers".

There was much waterfront activity at the time. Halifax port was particularly busy in the winter months when the Saint Lawrence River would freeze thus limiting the traffic at the port of Quebec. The ships brought war brides, refugees and European immigrants looking for better economic conditions. LeBlanc who by 1941 was Assistant Director General for Employment and Immigration, says the immigration department on the second storey of Pier 21 was constantly abuzz processing applications.

"After World War II, shiploads of immigrants would arrive, some without immigration papers. When this happened, it would create national attention, because a ship without immigration papers would need parliamentary approval for landing its passengers."

The government regulation of immigration through Halifax began with the first Canadian Immigration Act of 1869 which established an Immigration Office in that city. Although Canadian immigration records have been kept since 1865, the Halifax arrival schedules were not maintained until the city was officially declared a port of entry in January of 1881. Regrettably, no immigration records prior to 1881 are available.

Halifax harbour (top) in the fifties and Pier 21 today (right)

J.P. LeBlanc looks back on the years at Pier 21

Pier 21 had replaced Pier 2 whose facilities were largely destroyed in the Halifax Explosion of 1917. The processing of immigrants there for seven years thereafter was makeshift at best. But immigration numbers increased following First World War and necessitated a new immigration shed. LeBlanc says that in 1924 the situation was finally rectified. A new shed was opened adjoining the temporary southend railway station that for more than forty years would bear the name, familiar to hundreds of thousands of immigrants, *Pier 21.*

Pier 21 was a complex of buildings connected by ramps to the railway station with an infrastructure for immigration services, customs, health and welfare, agriculture, the Red Cross, a nursery, a hospital, a detention centre, a dining room and dormitories and an airing gallery or promenade overlooking the Halifax Harbour.

In the early part of the century, immigration to Canada was quite like the pattern of expatriate movement to the Arabian Gulf states that continues even to this day. It was very common for men to arrive alone, find employment, save their earnings and then bring their families over. Thus many women and children were out on their own crossing the Atlantic. Other than immigrants, there were the British Home Children that came too. The BHC movement was a well-intentioned but poorly executed humanitarian plan to relocate poor British children to Canadian farms as child labour. Although the movement began in the mid-1860s, it did not end until the Second World War. Thus as many as 100,000 children passed through Pier 21. From 1924 to 1930 immigration was brisk, though the depression of the 1930's would slow it considerably. Many immigrants who had arrived during these lean years became disillusioned and chose to return to Europe.

Canada entered the Second World War on September 10, 1939 and Pier 21 was immediately taken over by the Department of National Defence. Of the almost half a million servicemen and women who went overseas during the war, including those that departed from Pier 21, at least 50,000 would not live to return. Thousands would arrive back in Halifax on hospital ships like the *Letitia* and *Lady Nelson* throughout the war. During the war years Pier 21 saw the arrival of 3,000 British evacuee children. While Canadian officials refused to aid refugee children at the time, they did agree to let British children come as part of the CORB scheme (Children's Overseas Reception Board). Australia, New Zealand, South Africa and the United States also accepted children.

With hundreds of thousands of Canadian servicemen and women in Britain and continental Europe, wartime romances and marriages were inevitable. Consequently, 48,000 war brides and their 22,000 children began arriving during the war years with the largest influx disembarking at Pier 21 in 1946. Some brides came on small banana boats and others on luxury liners like the *Aquitania* and *Queen Mary*. The thousands of displaced people did not begin arriving in Canada until 1947. Canada was, in fact, less disposed to welcoming post-war immigrants at the time because of other priorities – especially having to put its economy back on its feet. One million Canadian men and women who had been employed in war industries had to find other work, and 975,000 personnel of the Canadian armed forces had to be absorbed into the post-war labour force.

These economic priorities were coupled with a strong anti-foreign sentiment as well. Canada had always had "preferred" and "non-preferred" groups when it came to immigration. British and American individuals were most favoured while central, eastern and southern Europeans were not. Some of the strongest voices against the acceptance of displaced people came from Quebec. In 1944 the Quebec Legislative Assembly passed a resolution threatening to boycott any post-war schemes of mass immigration. Many French Canadians looked upon immigration as an English Canadian policy designed to counteract Quebec's high birth rate as well as to ensure the pre-dominance of the English-speaking population. Consequently, Quebec's opposition did defer the development of a vigorous post-war immigration policy.

By 1946 Canada's economic paradigms improved and the

country's primary industries reported acute labour shortages especially in farming, forestry and mining. Thus pro-immigration pressure began to grow from industrialists and manufacturers as well as from the Canadian Pacific and Canadian National Railways. These efforts were rewarded in May of 1947 when Prime Minister Mackenzie King delivered his policy statement in the House of Commons. King acknowledged Canada's need for a larger population. He explained that Canada needed manpower for her primary industries and an increased population to defend its huge territory in a time of international insecurity. King said that: "Those immigrants who were admitted would be selected with care and only according to Canada's absorptive capacity."

As LeBlanc observes today, Canada has become far more generous. "At one time it did not like people from the Orient. It did not want Jewish immigrants. These policies needed legislative review and in time, our thinking on immigration became more generous."

The late 1940s and early fifties were the busiest years in the history of Pier 21. In addition to the hundred thousand refugees who arrived, were hundreds of immigrants from the Baltic states (Latvia, Lithuania and Estonia) who arrived illegally, fleeing Soviet oppression. Other Baltic citizens fled to Western Europe. Sweden, for example, accepted 22,000 Estonians between 1944 and the end of the war and integrated almost three-quarters into universities or into skilled occupations. However, as the Soviets pressured Sweden to turn the Baltic peoples over, many chose to flee in "little boats" like the *Walnut, Sarabande* and *Parnu*. These Baltic peoples who sailed to Canada were held in the detention quarters at Pier 21. All were eventually given landed immigrant status.

In the early 1950's many Dutch immigrants began to arrive seeking land which they could farm. Many of the most amusing Pier 21 stories come from the Dutch practice of importing homemade food to Canada - pepperoni, salami and cheeses of all kinds were favourites. But food brought by immigrants was confiscated and piled up in a heap in the middle of the hall at Pier 21, building a veritable mountain of sausages, loaves of bread, wheels of cheeses, fruits and other perishables.

"The immigration officer had the power to arrest," says LeBlanc. "If a shipping company allowed a passenger to board without immigration papers, it would be required to sail him back. These were inadmissibles. But there were others who came illegally too after World War II. The Displaced Persons were admitted, but detained until their admissibility was reviewed."

Canada's military, as he recalls, had sailed from Halifax for all of those wars : the Boer War, World War I and World War II.

But as the Chinese say, change is the only permanent thing. By the late sixties, more and more immigrants were choosing to fly to Canada rather than make the North Atlantic crossing by ship. Canadian immigration officers were splitting their time between meeting ships at Pier 21 and meeting planes at the airport. It was thus time to review Pier 21's position. On March 28, 1971, almost exactly forty-three years from its official opening, Pier 21 closed.

Not for long though. In 1989 a group of volunteers recognized that unless Pier 21 was preserved, a vital aspect of Canadian history would be lost. Inspired by LeBlanc, Pier 21 Society was formed. The mandate of Pier 21 Society was to transform Pier 21 into a facility of international importance, acknowledging the significance of immigration to the building of Canada and the creation of our cultural diversity. During these early stages one thing became clear: no matter what the future held for Pier 21, it would always remain in the hearts and memories of the people who had arrived there.

But reservations about the scope of this historic monument remain as people ask why should Pier 21 confine itself to history. Immigration is Canada's lifeblood. It's an on-going saga and Pier 21 must reflect that reality.

On July 1, 1999 their efforts paid off when the $9 million Pier 21 National Historic Site opened to the public. The mandate was to honour all those who set foot on Canadian soil through its gateway.

But reservations about the scope of this historic monument remain as people ask why should Pier 21 confine itself to history. Immigration is Canada's lifeblood. It's an on-going saga and Pier 21 must reflect that reality. None should be led to thinking that the society celebrates the mostly European immigrant flow through Pier 21. Why do we have to leave this celebration at history's door? Ruth Goldbloom, the current President of Pier 21 Society observed rightly once: "Whether we came here 300 years ago or only a few years ago, we all came for the same reasons, whether that be poverty, persecution or the desire for a new life."

Pier 21 commemorates the bravery of immigrants and refugees who fled war, persecution and instability to make a new life in Canada. But this isn't history. People are still leaving – or being driven from – their homes for these reasons. That is the point being made.

LeBlanc who talked to this writer a month prior to the book's publication agrees somewhat. He says while Pier 21 Society's mandate was precisely to honour those who came through its gateway, perhaps there is reason to expand that mandate today. "Pier 21 Society does not want to be an advisor to the government on immigration nor does it want to embroil itself in policy analysis. But I think one must find a way to make it reflect the significance of the ongoing immigration process to Canada."

In the process, we shall forever honour the people who come, make Canada their home and together enrich this nation.

The SOS and the Red Cross. Give them a hand.

The million or more immigrants that came to Canada via Pier 21 between 1928 and 1971 came with their dreams, others fleeing war, and some others cherishing a reunion. There were challenges in welcoming these people who spoke another language, were traumatised, lost their children at sea and so on. But on board Pier 21, were the presence of volunteer groups like the Red Cross, Sisters of Service and the Jewish Immigrant Aid Society.

Sr. Liota says there were sad occasions and jubilant ones. "There were occasions when passengers would arrive after burying their children or relatives at sea."

The mandate of the Sisters of Service (SOS) was to receive and welcome newcomers to Canada in the name of the church and the country and assist them in their integration and adaptation to Canadian society, says Sr. Patricia Burke, the Archivist at SOS. "The sisters provided reception services at the Ports of Halifax, Saint John, New Brunswick, Quebec City and Montreal. Sisters of Service hostels in the major cities provided a base for support services for newcomers, particularly women, assisting them in finding employment, counseling, language training and so on," she says. It's unfortunate that the Sisters of Service are not currently involved in immigration or refugee work.

Sr. Sally Liota who was out there for fifteen years from 1955 to 1969 interpreted for thousands of immigrants while on the job picking up Spanish, French, German and even Hungarian.

"When the Hungarian refugees came along, one could see they were already traumatized, fleeing the communist regime at the time and apprehensive about how they would be received in Canada. It was important that we spoke some Hungarian. It made them feel at home," she says.

Sr. Liota says there were sad occasions and jubilant ones. "There were occasions when passengers would arrive after burying their children or relatives at sea," Sr. Liota recalls. "We had to deal with trauma and provide comfort. Archbishop Hayes would provide Chaplaincy service at the time and we would assist him."

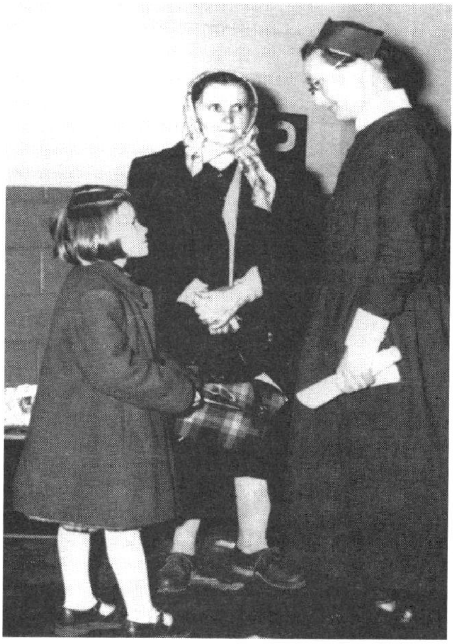

Left: Sr. Sally Liota of the Sisters of Service helps immigrants get settled on the "immigrant Trains" circa 1950.
Right: Sister Kelly welcomes groups of new arrivals to the Pier. Photo courtesy: Sisters of Service

The Sisters of Service operate an Information Booth at Pier 21. Circa 1950
Photo courtesy: SOS

But there were jubilant times as well, when babies would be born on ship and would be given lifetime free passage or when prospective grooms would arrive for reunions with their brides.

People would come with all their possessions, says Sr. Liota. "They brought their beds, their pots and pans and foods preserved in oil or vinegar – even salami and dried meats – which of course would be confiscated. Many brought along their dogs and some refused to have them quarantined."

"The biggest challenge," says Ruddick "was to stay on our feet, sometimes all night and day."

Often times the Sisters of Service would be called to attend on the sick or to escort them to hospitals. "We were on call 24 hours. Some of the ships would call at night and each of them would bring any where between 2,000 to 3,000 immigrants," Sr. Lioto says.

The SOS mission was founded in 1922 mainly to serve immigrants who were settling in Western Canada. It opened two hospitals at the time. But after World War II, the SOS worked for Displaced Persons (DPs), as well, arranged employment for many of them and provided assistance in their settlement. In many ways, the SOS was also bringing the faith to the many Catholics who were settling down in the prairies.

The Red Cross deserve a hand too. From January 1946 to January 1947, some 45,000 war brides and children from the British Isles, Holland and Italy entered Canada through Pier 21. Kay Ruddick, a young escort officer with the Red Cross, at the time, says she did 15 trips across the Atlantic to bring home war brides. "Our job was to provide care to women and children and to refer the sick to the army doctors and nurses on board the ship," she says.

"The biggest challenge," says Ruddick "was to stay on our feet, sometimes all night and day. For instance, on the Queen Mary we once had a terrible storm. The waves hit the bridge and came down into the Captain's cabin and through the portholes washed passengers out of their bunk beds. So many were sick.... even the electrical system went out of commission until the morning."

Ruddick says the experience was terrifying. "This was before the Queen ships had stabilizers and which is why there were fears of the ship capsizing. It just tossed all night, bow to stern and sideways." But she says in the end, the price paid was worth it. "When the ship pulled into Pier 21, it was heartening to see excited brides looking for familiar faces on the dock."

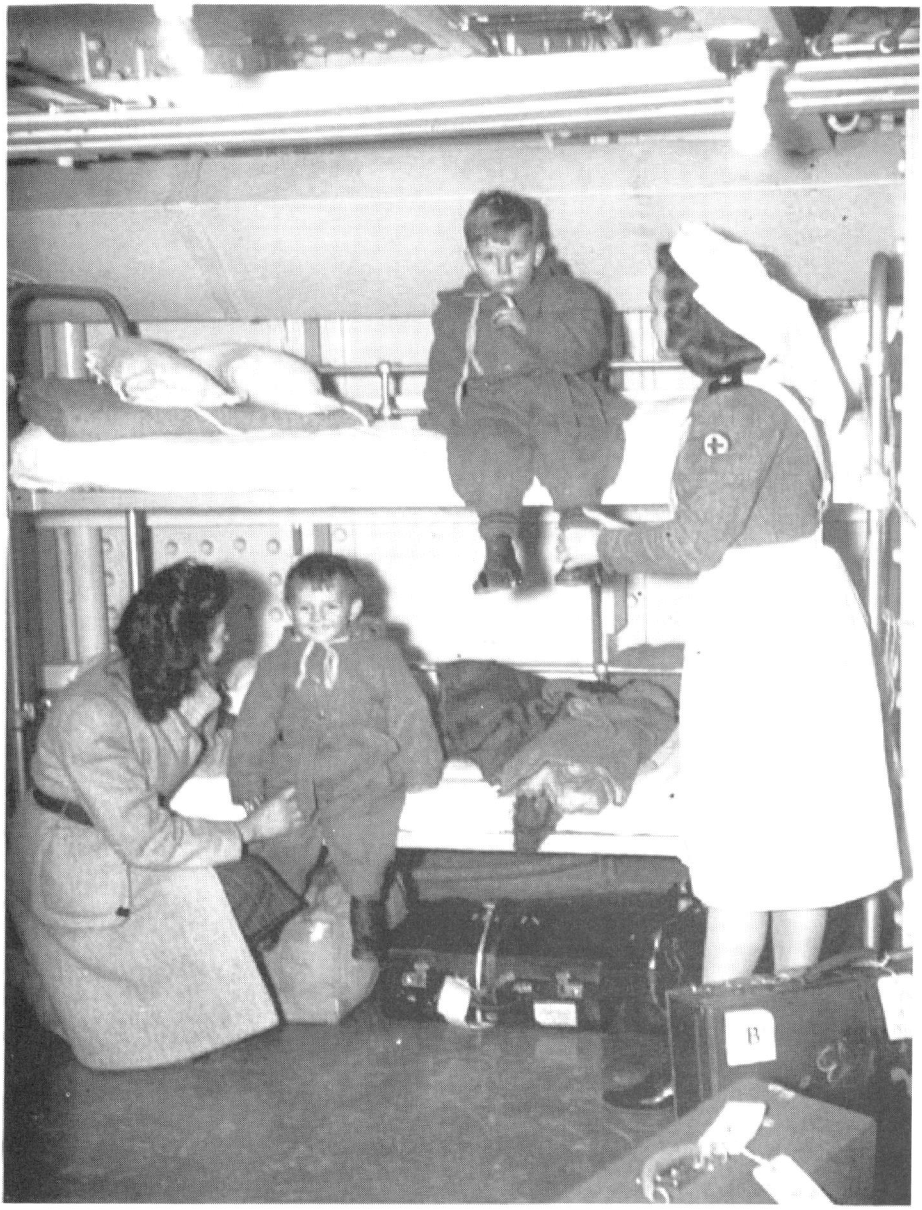

The Red Cross gave children care on board the ships

Arrival of the Aquitania at Halifax.

Escort Officer Kay (Douglas) Ruddick (in a 1946 photo) did 15 escort trips across the Atlantic bringing home war brides

Immigration officer, Frank Wright, recounts memories of his job at Pier 21 in the 1950s

Frank Wright, an immigration officer at Pier 21, started out as security guard in 1948 when he returned from the war. As he recalls today, Pier 21 had accommodation and detention quarters. Those quarters, which included a hospital managed by doctors and nurses accommodated anywhere between 300-350 people. Wright's job was to ensure the safe custody of the people there. "At one time, in addition to those quarters, I was responsible for an additional 800 people housed in the Old Rock Prison Hospital," he says.

Wright remembers that back in the early fifties, immigration had to deal with the first defector off a Russian ship. "Our quarters at Pier 21 were not prison camps," says Wright. "But of course, defectors were not free to leave our quarters, because the ships crew could come and seize them." He says he remembers a time when three Bulgarians gave themselves up to him. He took a bunch of particulars from them and later gave them a ship to go and rest. But after a while when they did not show up, he got to know that ship's crew had come in and taken them away.

"So we had to be very careful about leaving people out. Sometimes we kept them in custody for their own protection, and they didn't want to go anyway.

Wright says that in the those days immigration had to deal with several Polish defectors too, whose ships would come to port for supplies. "They would abandon their ships and ask for asylum. The Greeks would not defect, but desert their ships and seek employment with Greek companies in Canada." Later Wright would do escort jobs taking ship's deserters to Montreal.

Wright, who began boarding ships as early as in 1908 when his father joined immigration says the challenge of the job for an immigration officer was to make people welcome. "The first impression is an everlasting one and so we took time out to welcome people."

Immigration staff at the time were veterans of the war who had spent many years overseas. Having witnessed communism and Nazism in action, veterans saw what these people had lived through and how afraid they were of government officers. "Right after the war these people were terrified. You knew it from the look on their faces when they came off the ships," Wright says.

Immigrants at the time came not only with their hopes and dreams but with all their possessions, other than a kitchen sink. The processing of immigrants was a challenge as well. "One day we had 3,800 immigrants arrive in twenty-four hours," Wright recalls. "Thirty-eight hundred people were processed landed immigrants in one day." He says officers checked immigration papers when immigrants got off the ship to ensure, firstly, that everyone had a valid vaccination certificate. "In the old days everyone had to have a vaccination certificate and a valid passport. Their immigration papers were issued to them overseas. The only criteria at the time, after the war, was that the immigrant had to be in good health and of good character. The Immigration Officer would go over the form verifying with the immigrant that the information was correct.

Frank Wright (left) with Mike Trenaman in the 1940s

The officer would then notify the various religious groups of the destinations of these people who would notify a minister, priest, rabbi, in all those cities of Canada. "In that way, someone from the clergy would come to meet with the newcomer to Canada and help was at hand," says Wright.

He recalls with some humor

the fact that the immigrants who came always hesitated to declare their money. "The people were accustomed to seeing government officials in their countries take bribes. So even though they tucked away their cash in a little bag and hid it on their person, they hated to declare their money. After we were able to convince them of our good intentions, they would dig down into their clothes for the little bag."

Wright says that after the war, it was illegal to bring more than $10 into Canada because of the black marketeering and hoarding of dollars. But some immigrants, he says, tried to get around that regulation. He recounts a humorous tale: "Pier 21 then had two rooms. One room was for assembly. There we had wooden benches where we seated people. One day I saw blood spilling from the bench and went to investigate. It was a Jewish man. He was bleeding from his rectum. So we took him to the other room where we had two doctors to examine him. They stripped him off his pants and were shocked at what they saw. The doctor came to me and said :'I think we've hit a gold mine'. The man had stuffed 100 dollar bills in his rectum because of the regulation limiting import of dollars into Canada.

Wright recalls some poignant observations from Dutch immigrants: "Many Dutch came after the war," he says. "Go across Nova Scotia, down through the valley and see those farms. They would come with large families. There was one Dutch family with eighteen children. When the immigration officer turned to the father and asked: 'What do you plan to do in Canada?' the father said: 'I want to start all over again.' The officer looked down the row of eighteen children and thought to himself: this man must really be ambitious."

The Greeks, he recalls, would bring in octopus tied in cloth. I remember people moving away from one Greek man holding their noses because his octopus had gone bad.

The recognition of immigrant credentials which is a matter of grave concern for immigrant settlement organizations even today was a stumbling block in those years as well. Consequently, many came to Canada to work as domestics. "There could have been at least fifty young girls on every ship coming to Canada to work as domestics," says Wright. "They would be detained in our quarters overnight. It must have been rather frightening for them I would imagine. Indeed, they had work contracts with Canadians - but what could be done if they chose to pursue employment elsewhere?"

Wright says his wife who was a nurse came to Canada as a domestic because the authorities would not recognize her credentials in Canada. "She was told she would have to go back to Europe and train another year. She did go back to Germany and there they thought she was crazy, that we were crazy in Canada, because she was a top nurse."

Once medical examinations were carried out , officers would send immigrants to a large ramp where they proceeded to customs. The Sisters of Service, United Church and the Red Cross were there to provide assistance. "They would give them a box of goodies while they waited for a train to depart for other provinces."

Looking back, Wright says immigration is no place for a man or woman who has no liking for people. "I would tell the young fellows then that if they were not people-oriented, get the hell out of here. You are not only hurting people, you are hurting yourself working with something you don't like." He says that over the years people have demonstrated much gratitude. "I would get that gratitude frequently going around Halifax to the Greek stores, Italian stores, the German stores, Lebanese stores.

When they saw us come in to eat, they would not want us to pay for the meal. But we had to tell them that working as public servants we could not accept gratuities."

At 83 today, Wright volunteers for a Seniors organizations in Vancouver and is on the executive legion of the Federal Superannuates of Canada which has 400,000 members.